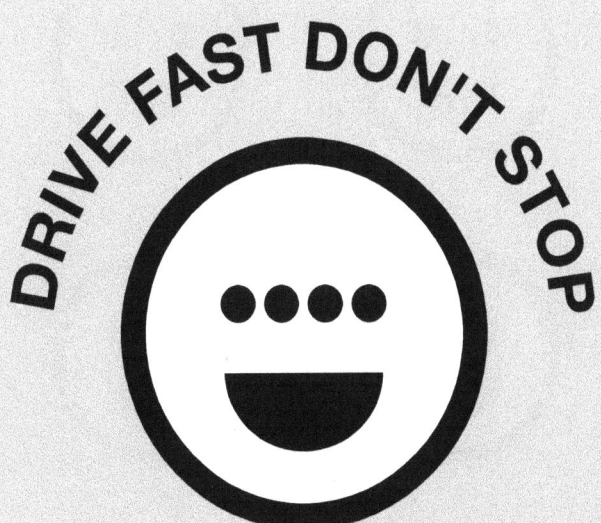

DRIVE FAST DON'T STOP

4

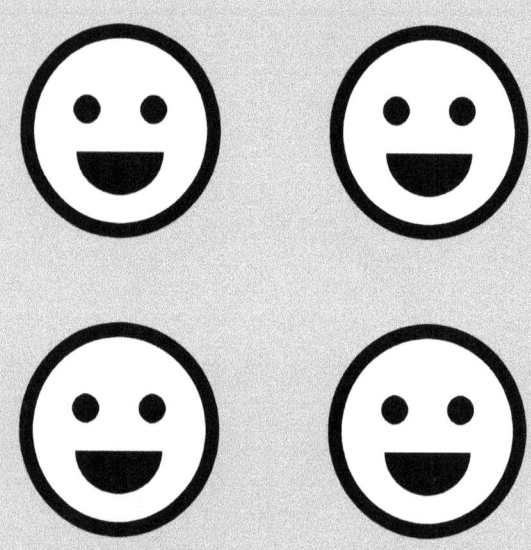

DRIVE FAST DON'T STOP

BOOK FOUR

A RANDOM ASSORTMENT
OF AUTOMOBILES

FAST DON'T

FAST DON'T

E FAST DON'T :

VE FAST DON'T ST

RIVE FAST DON'T STO

DRIVE FAST DON'T STOP

DRIVE FAST DON'T STOP

DRIVE FAST DON'T STOP

AUTOMOBIL

AUTOMOBILE

AUTOMOBILES

AUTOMOBILES

AUTOMOBILES

AUTOMOBILES

AUTOMOBILES

AUTOMOBILES

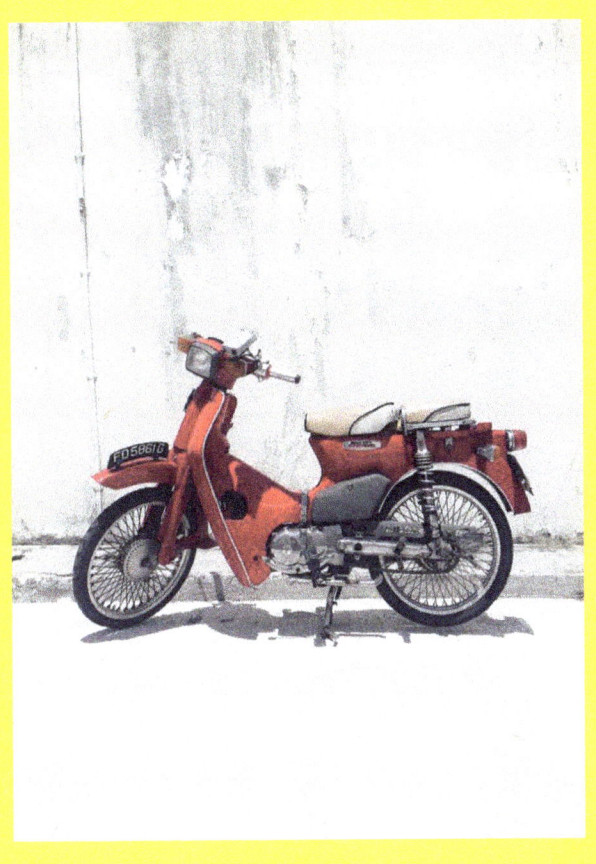

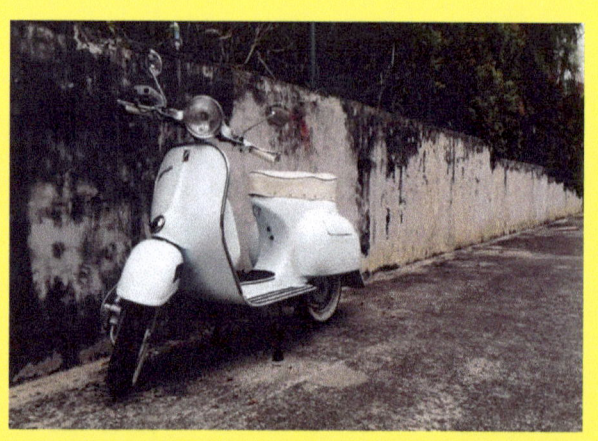

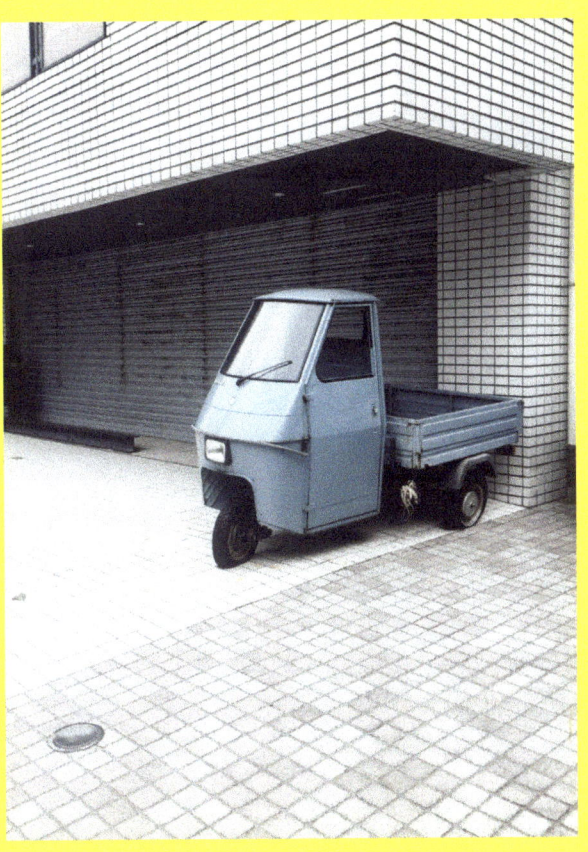

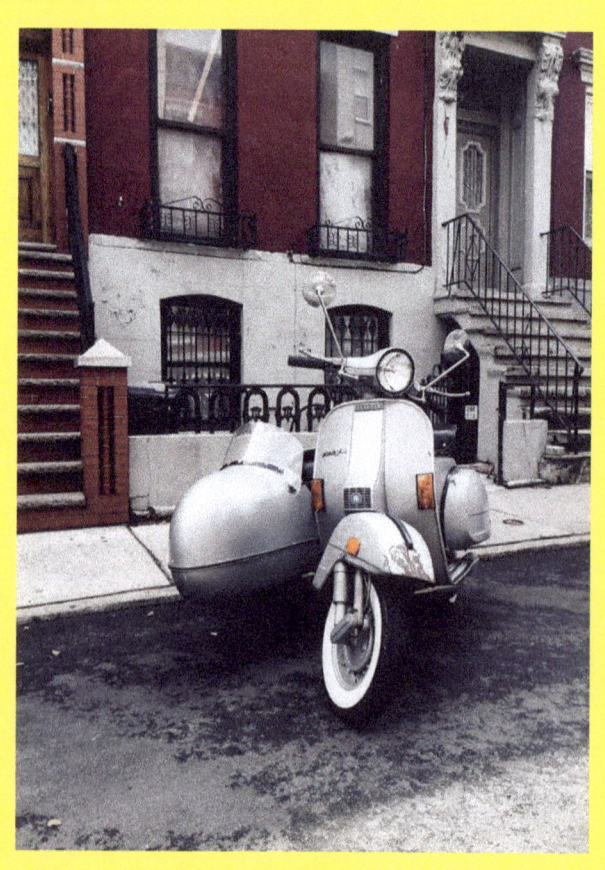

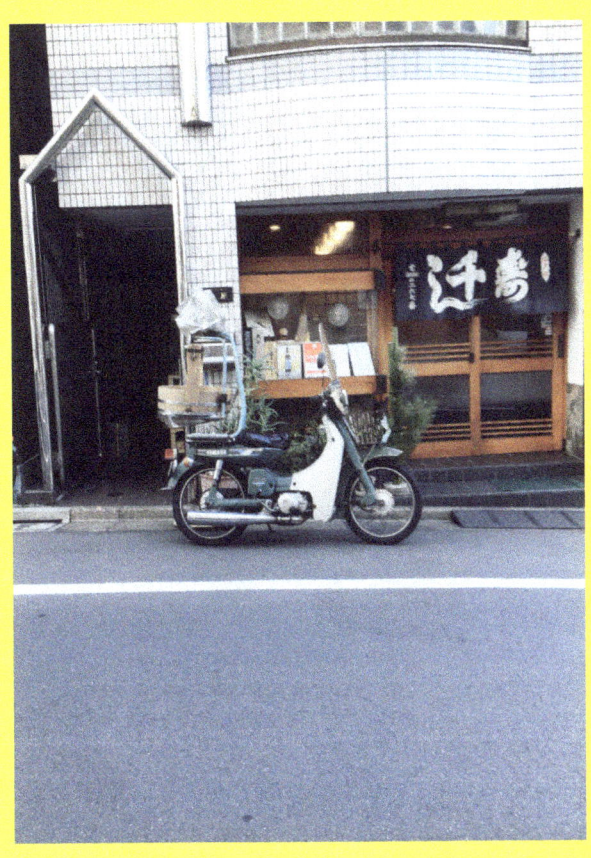

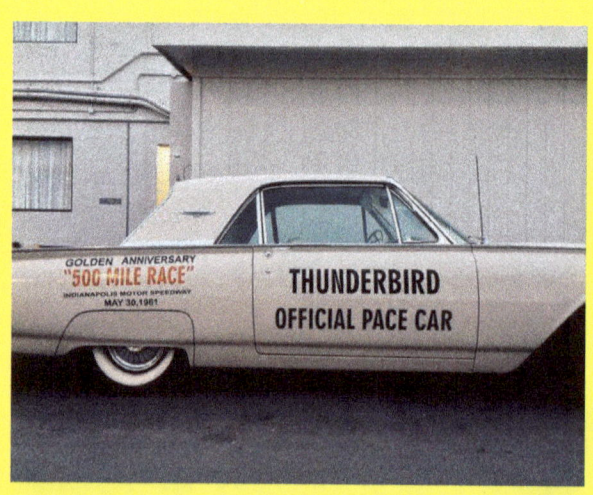

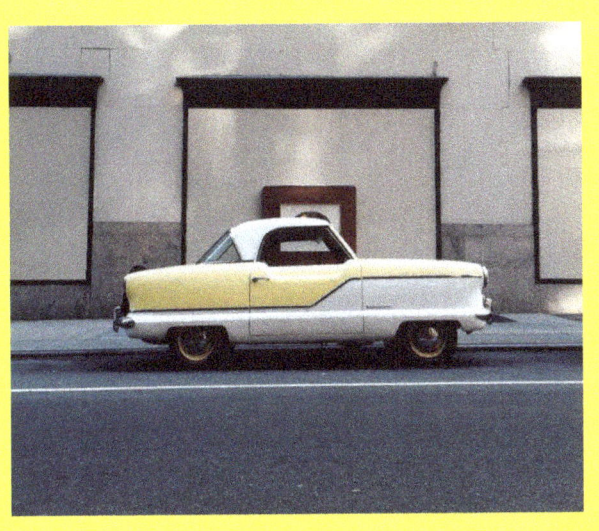

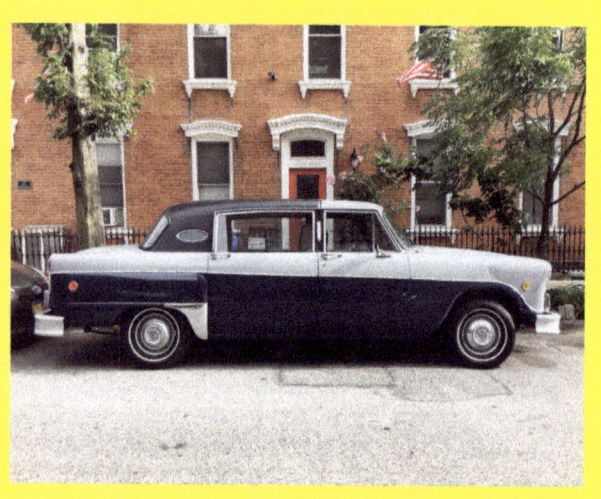

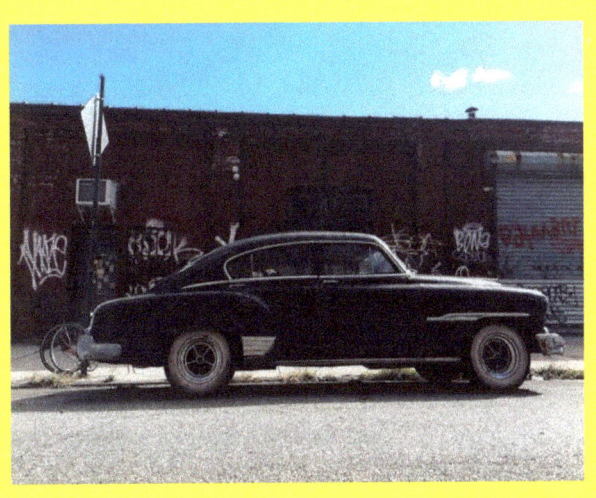

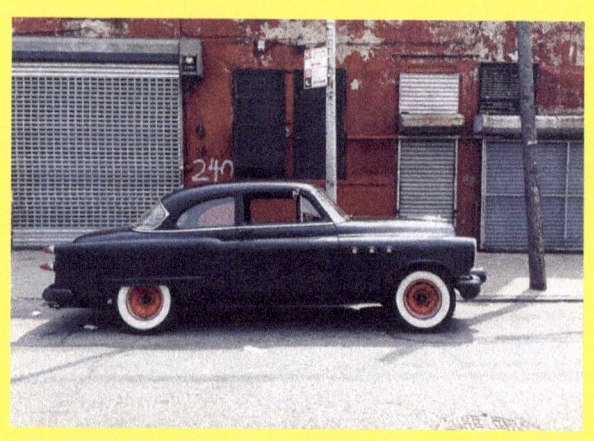

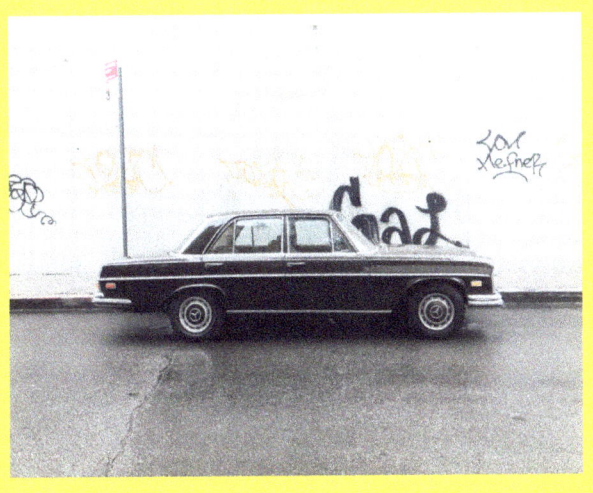

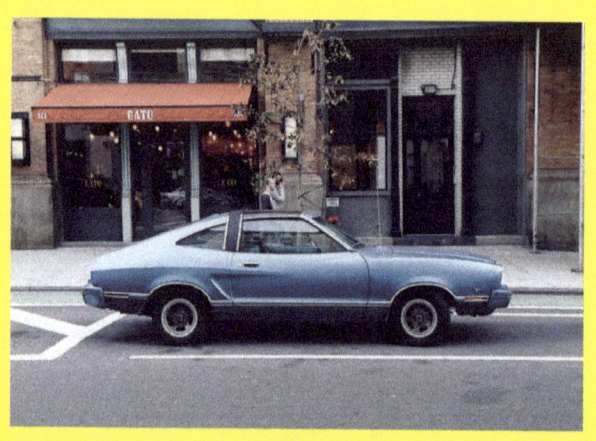

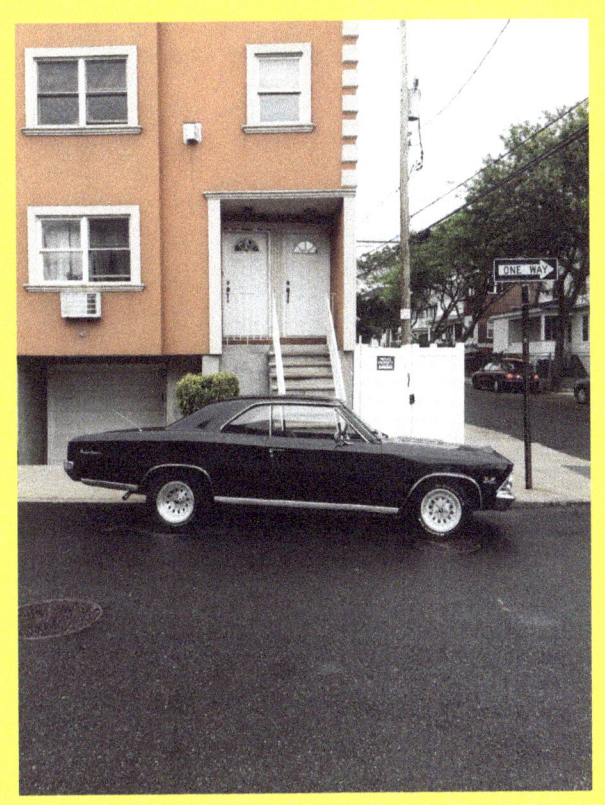

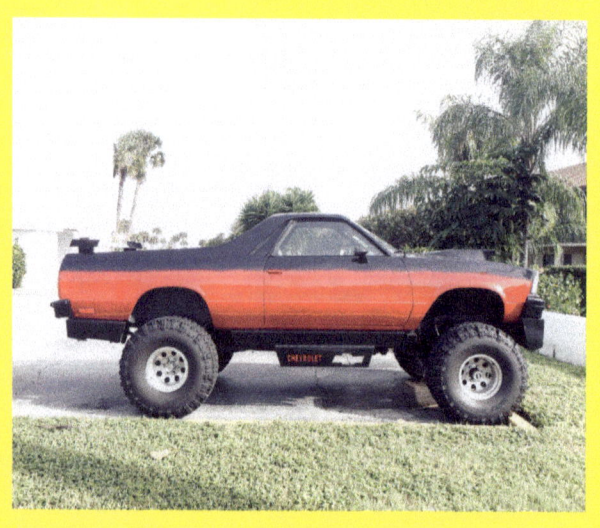

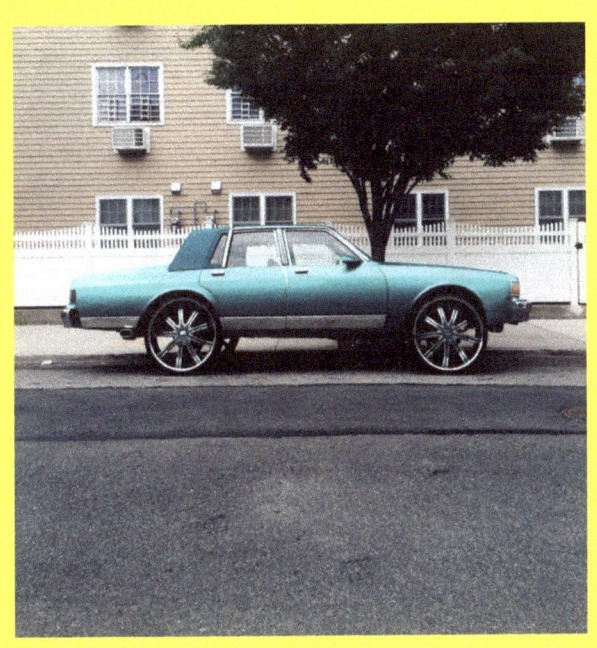

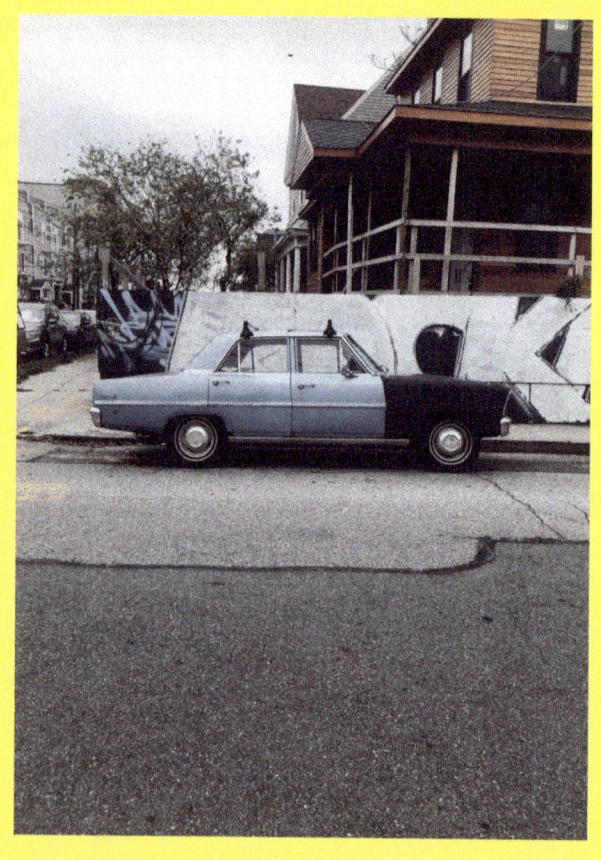

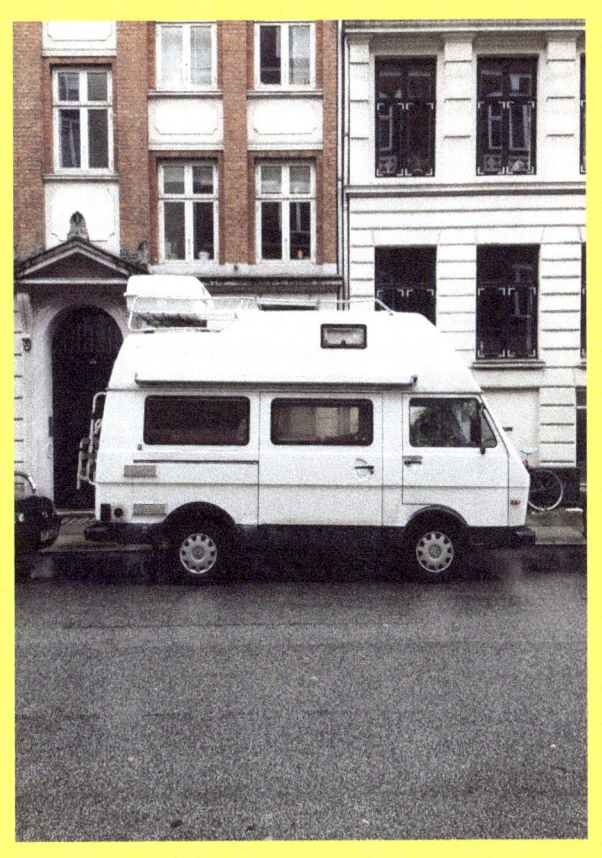

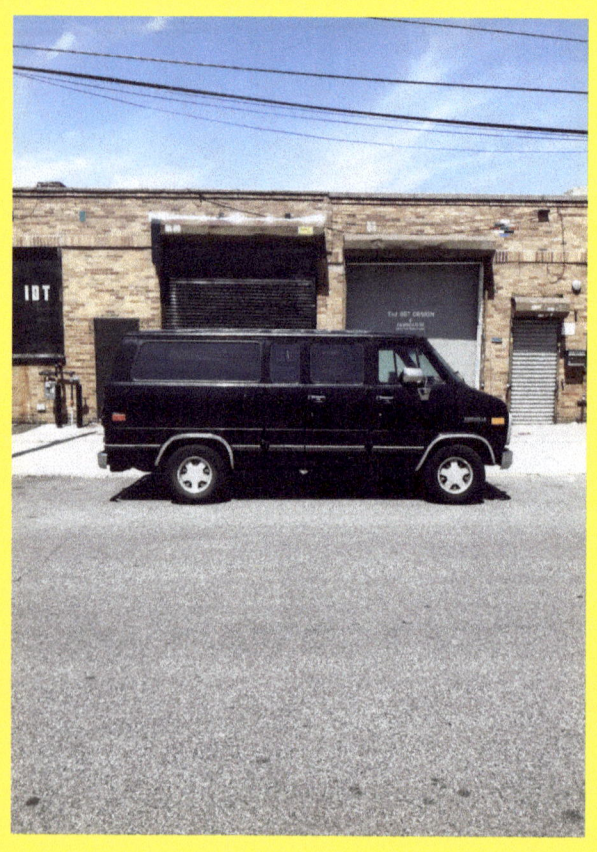

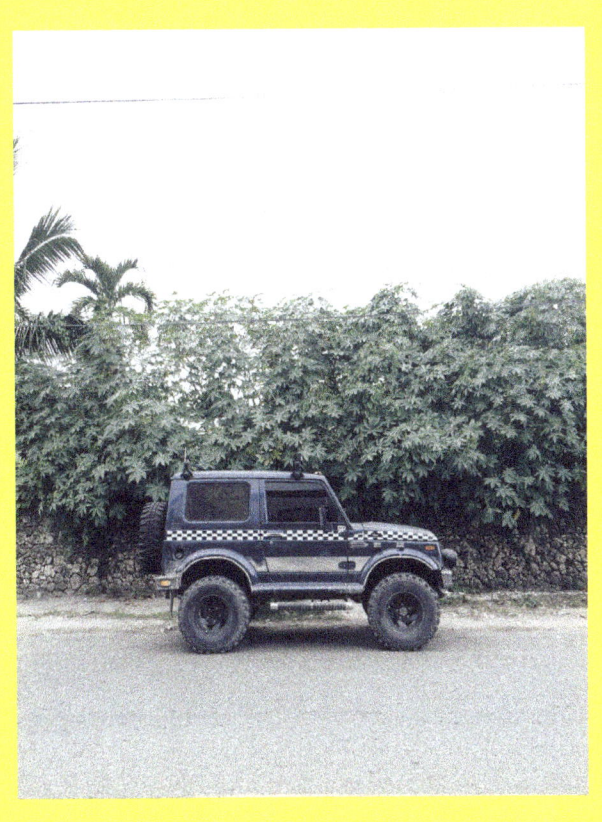

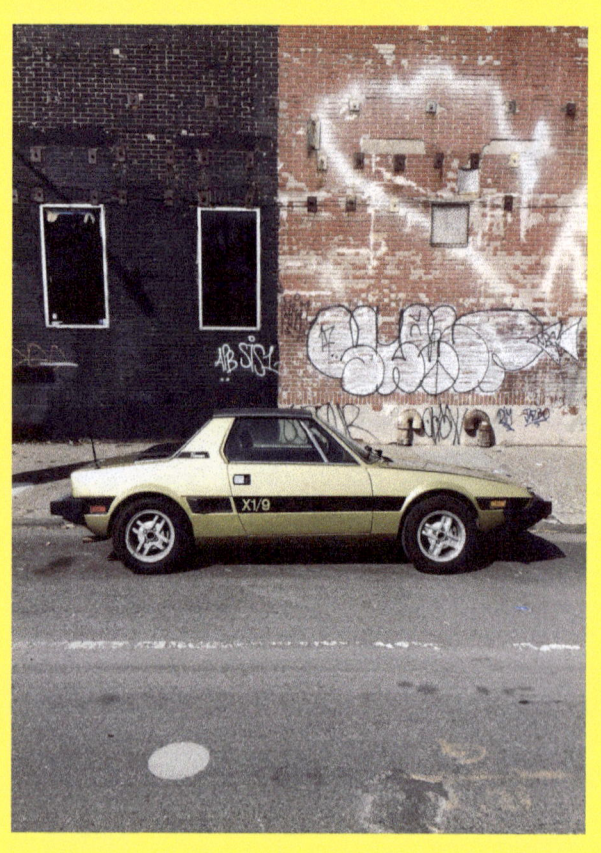

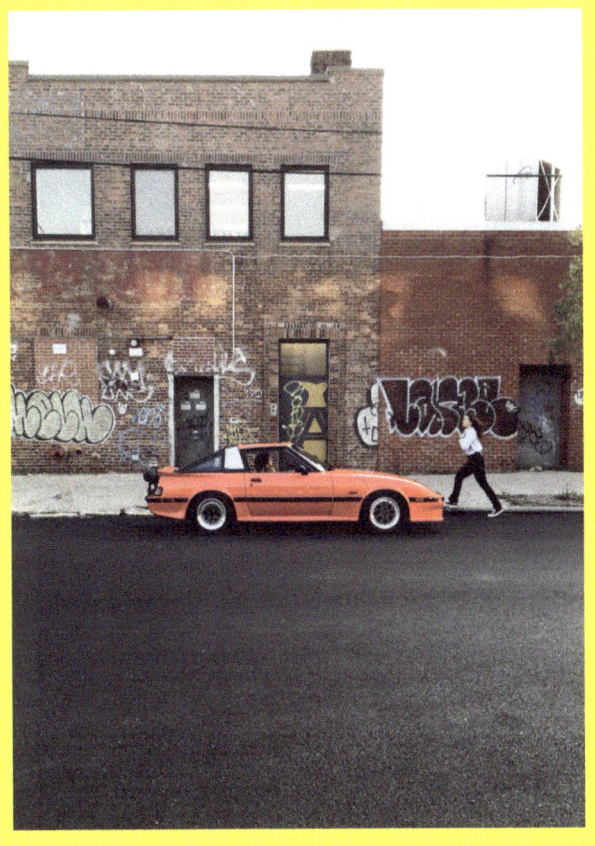

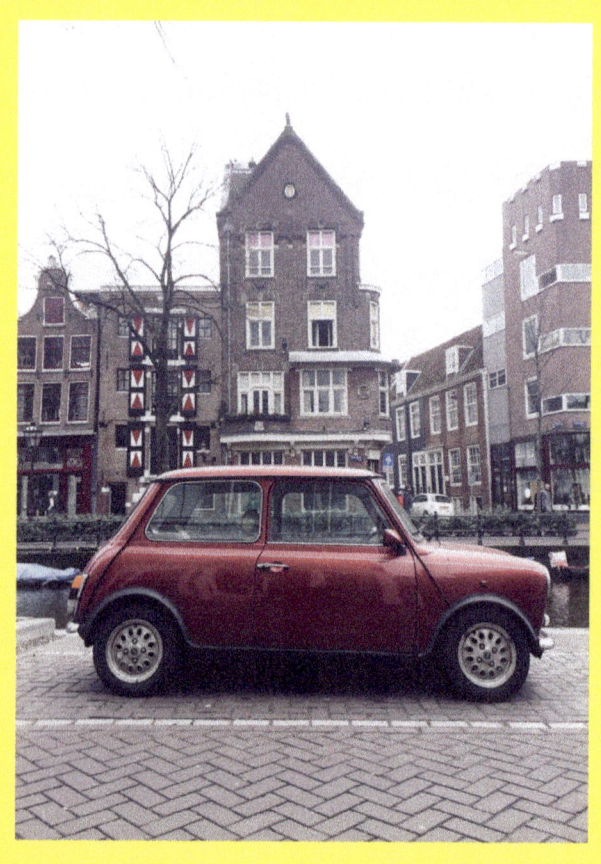

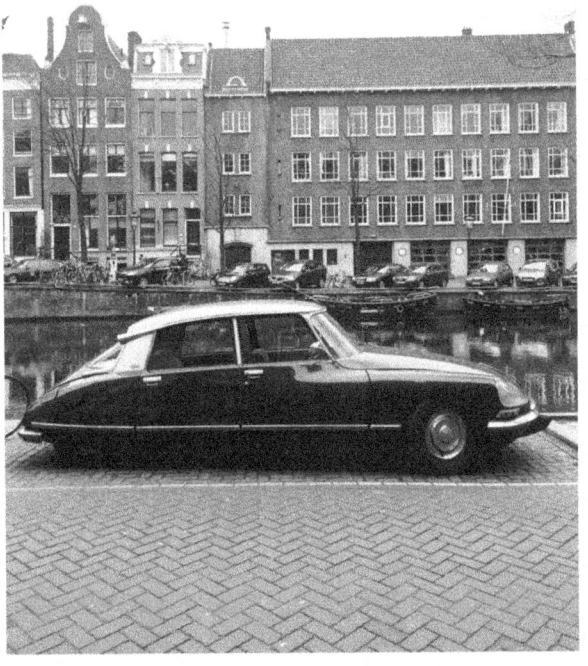

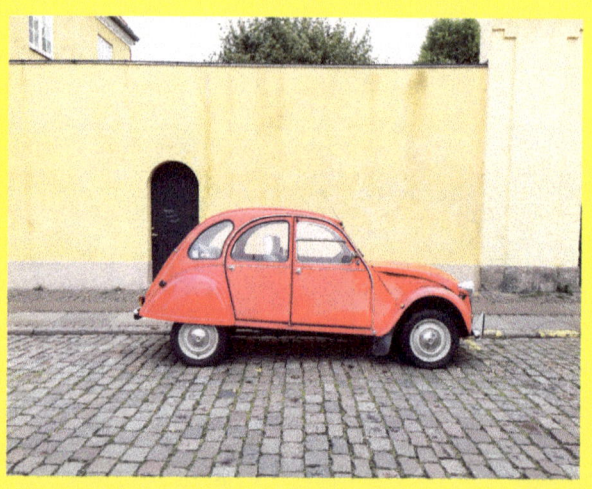

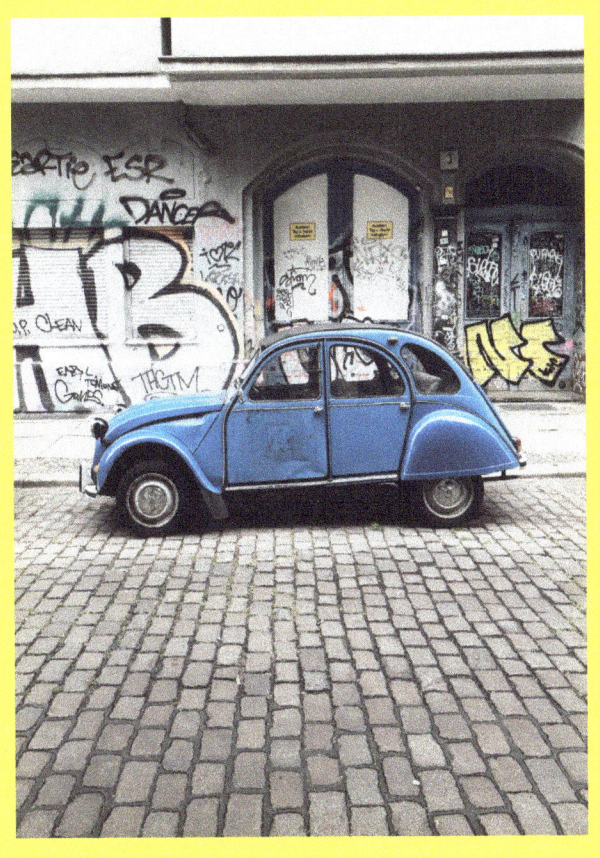

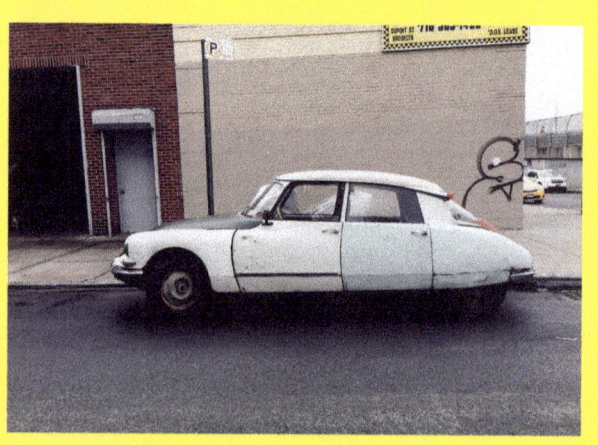

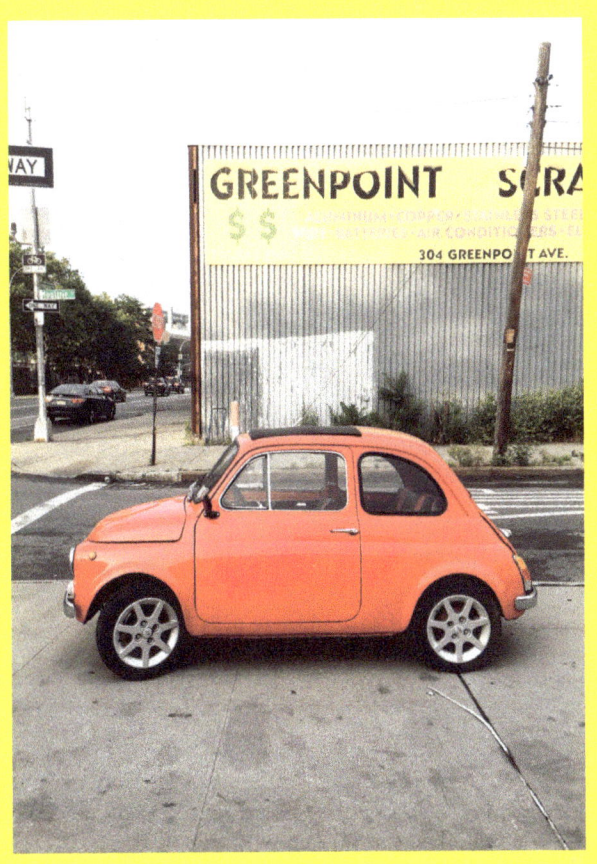

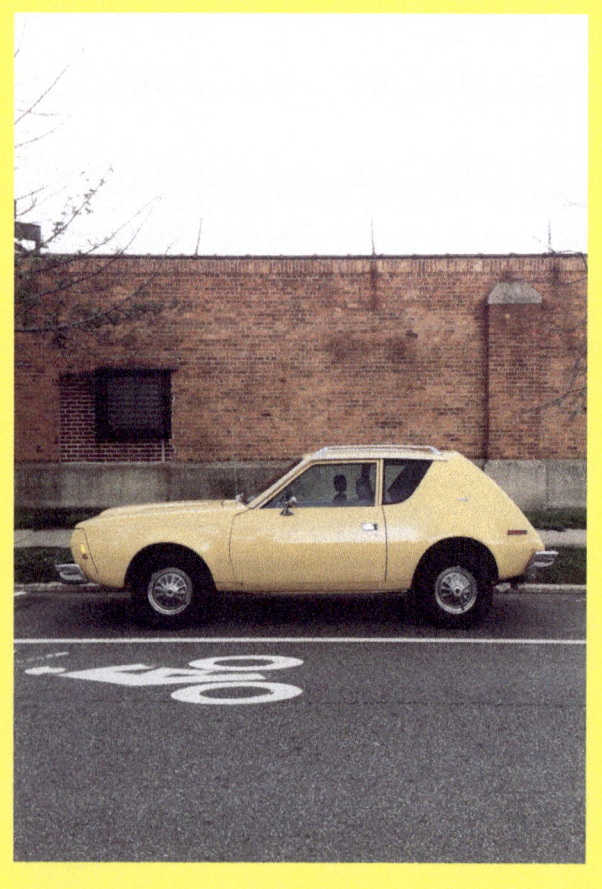

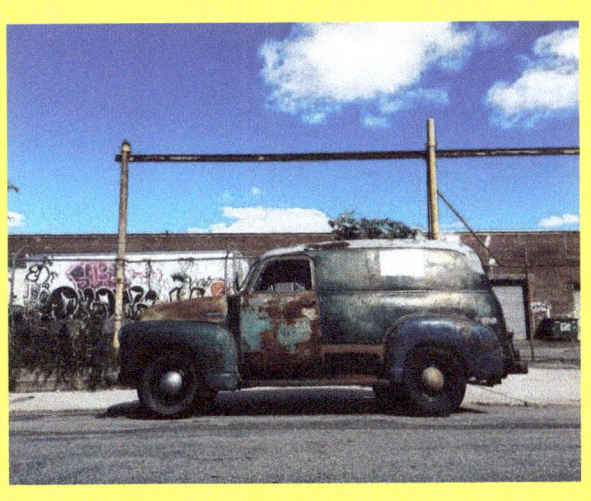

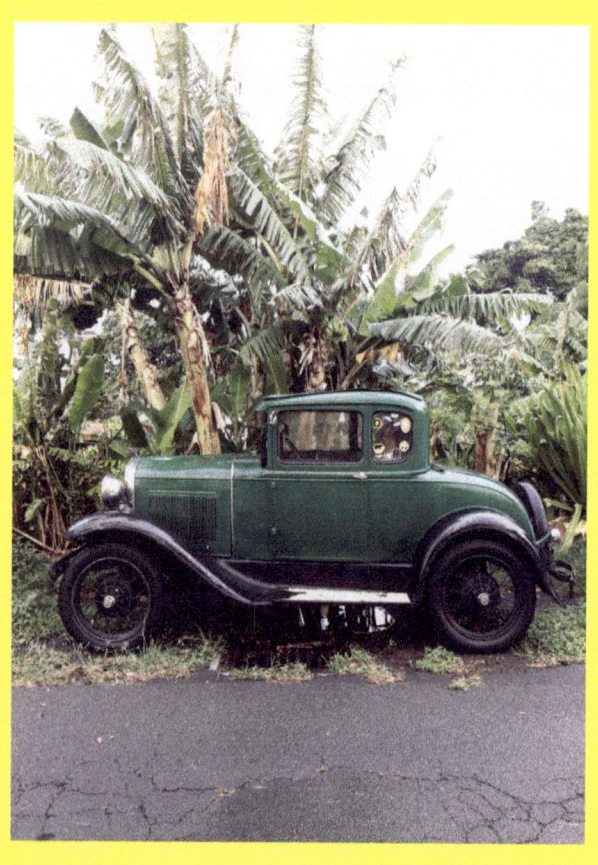

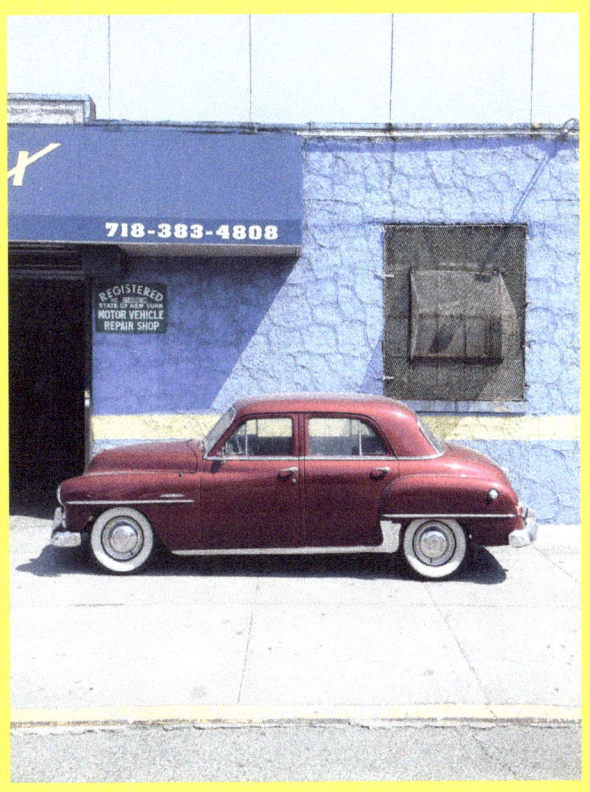

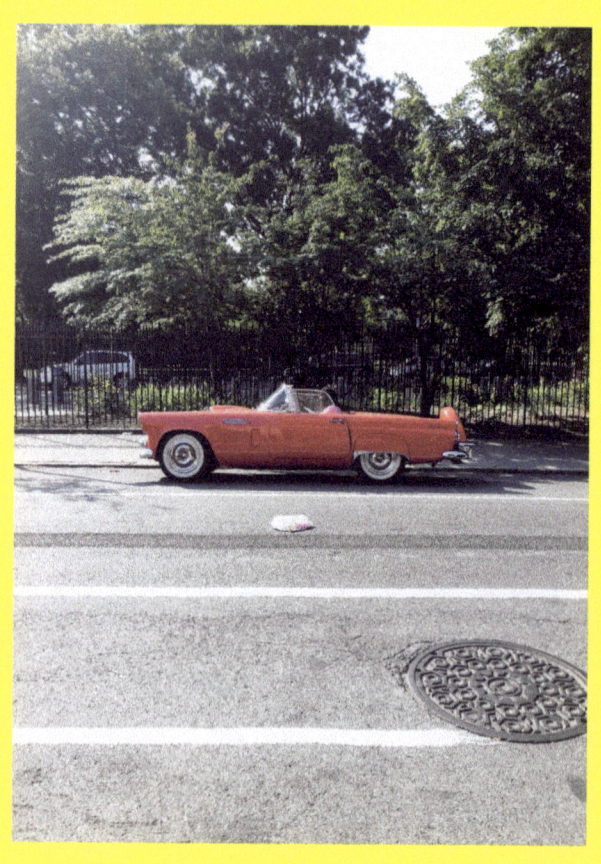

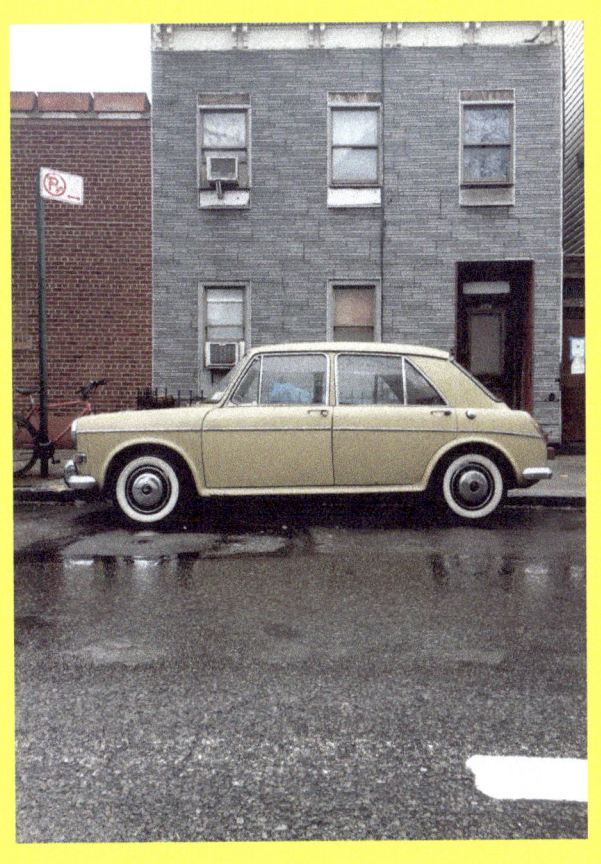

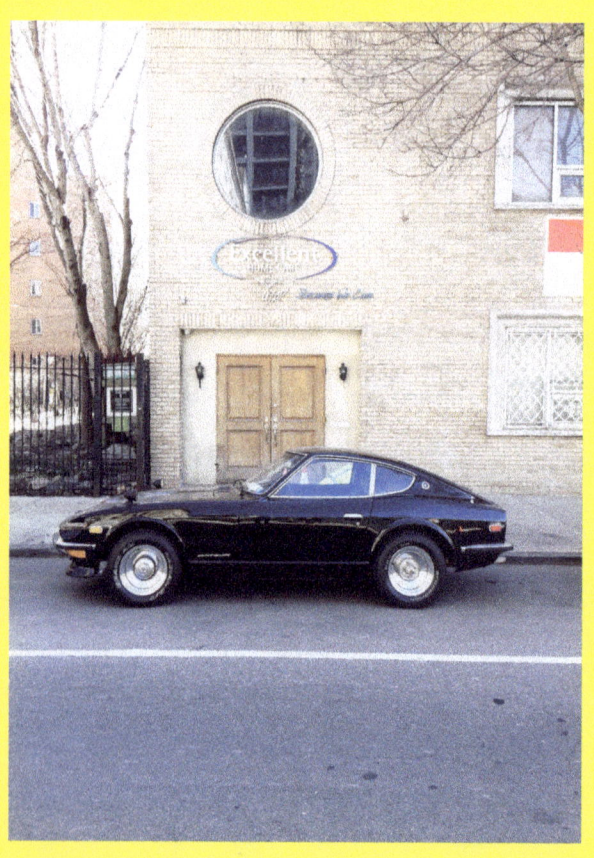

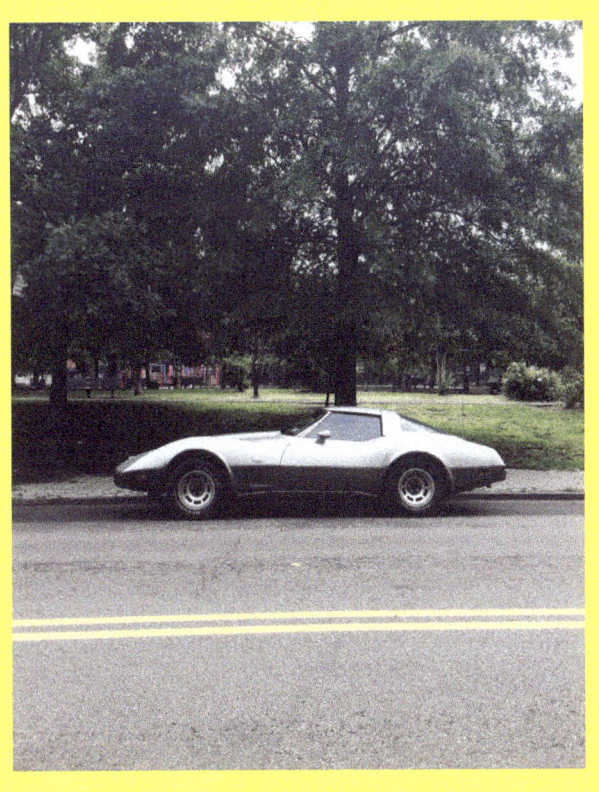

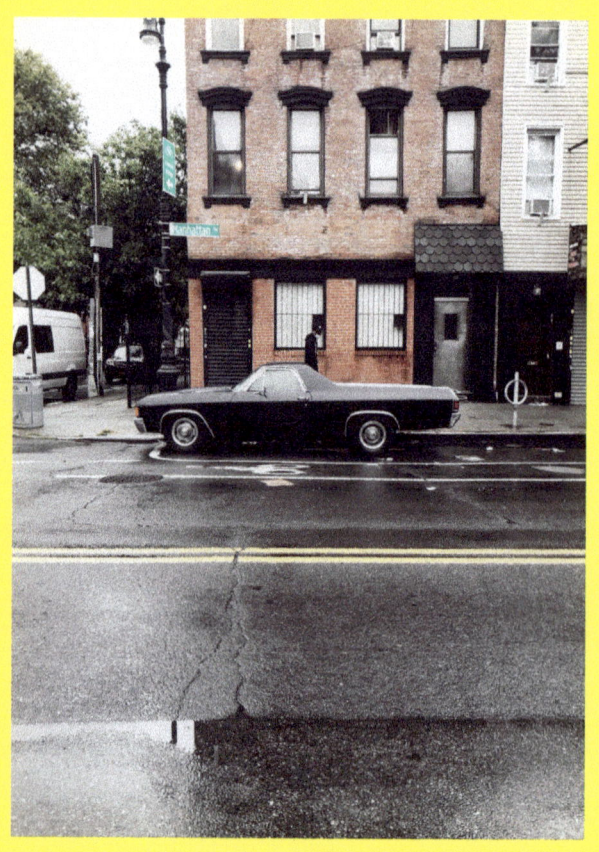

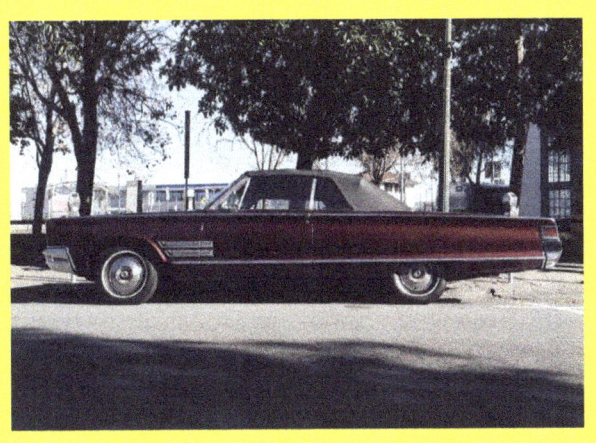

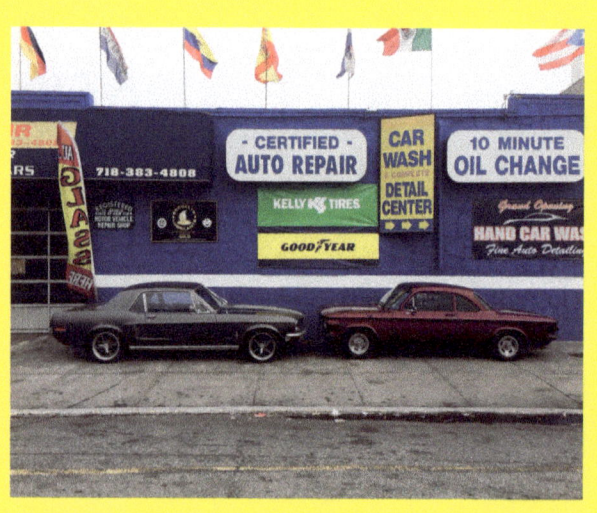

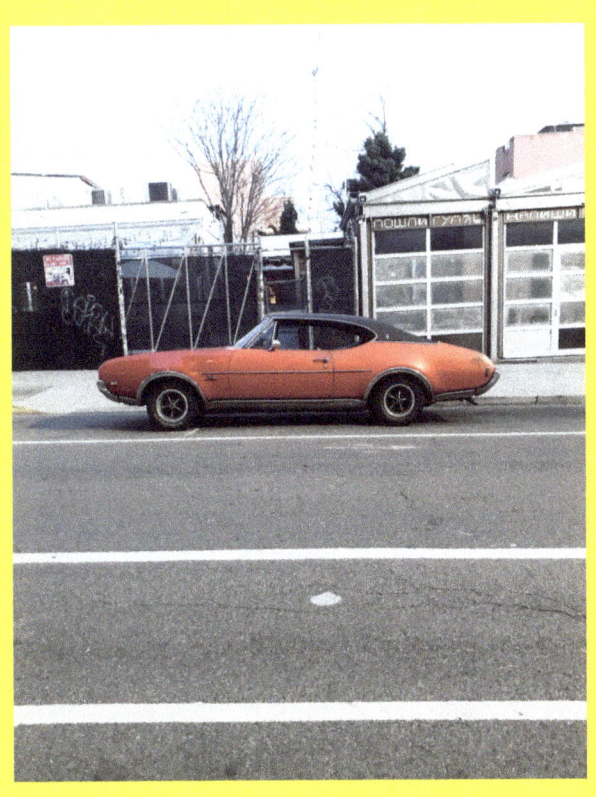

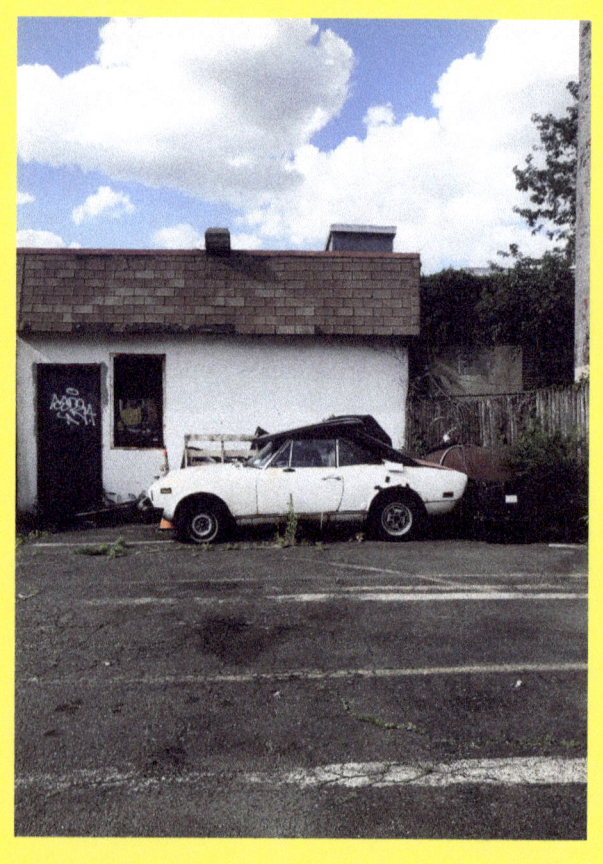

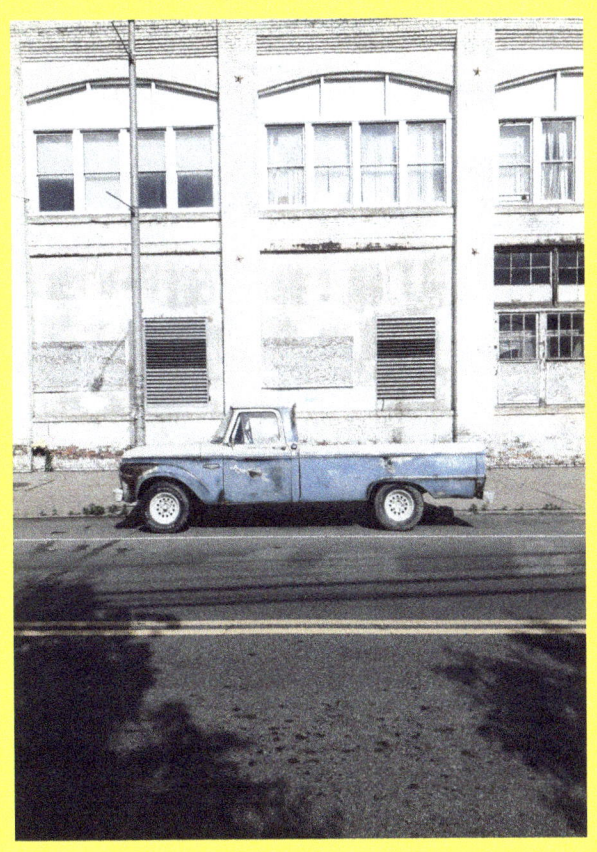

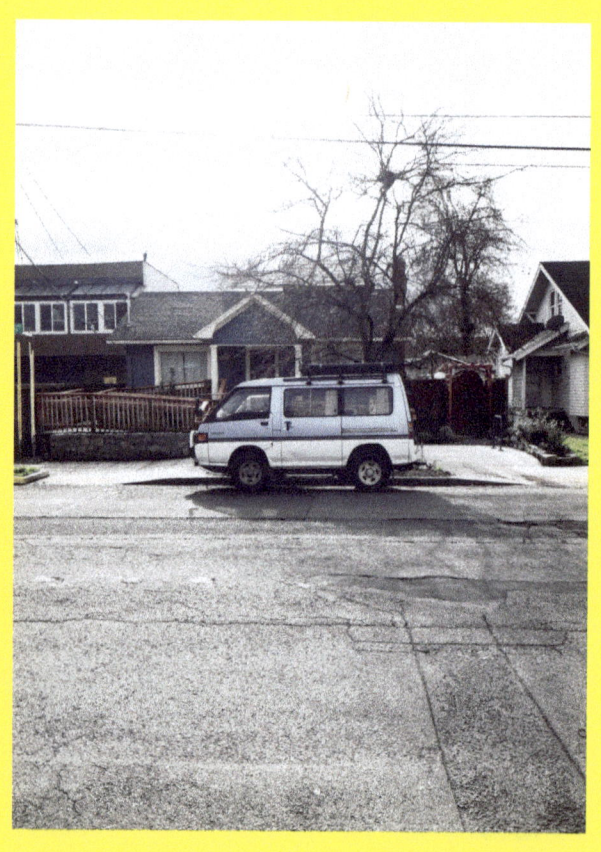

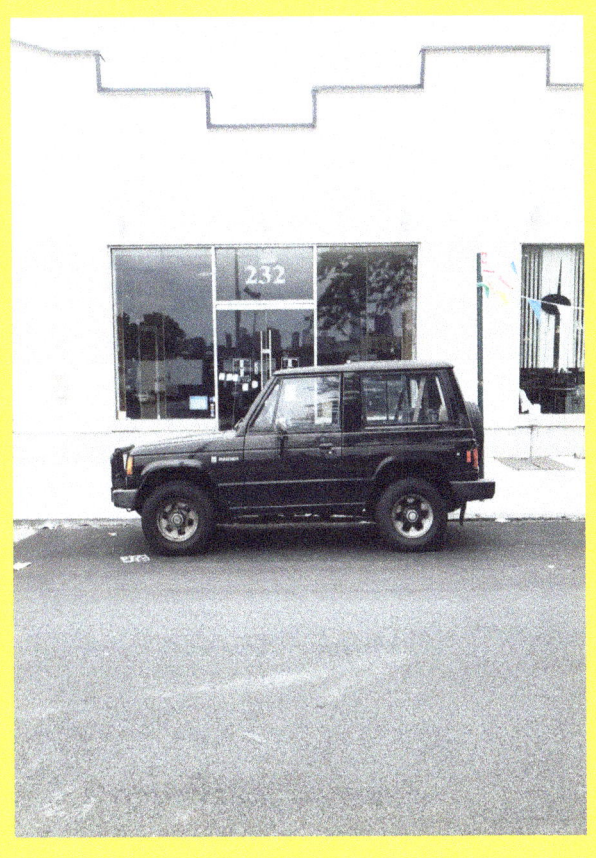

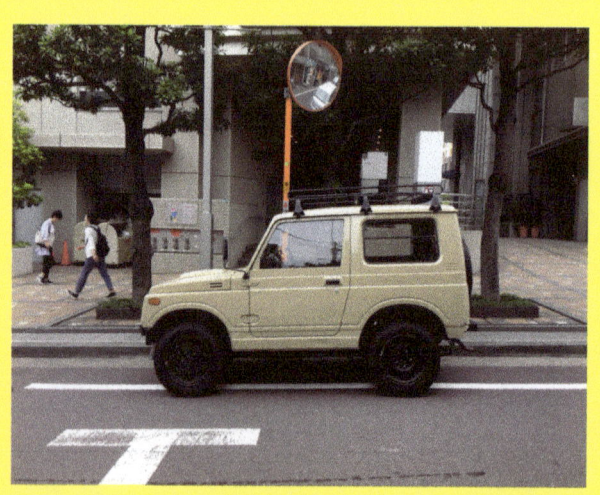

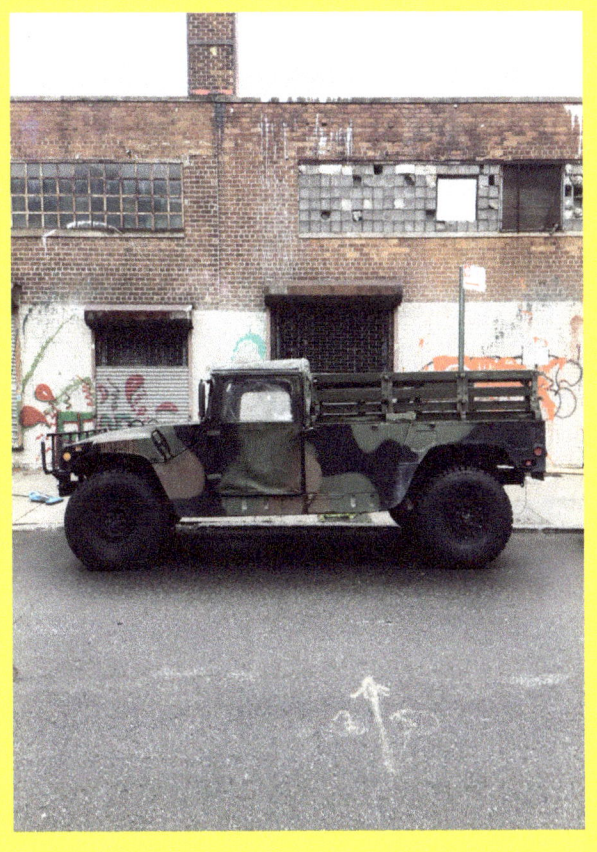

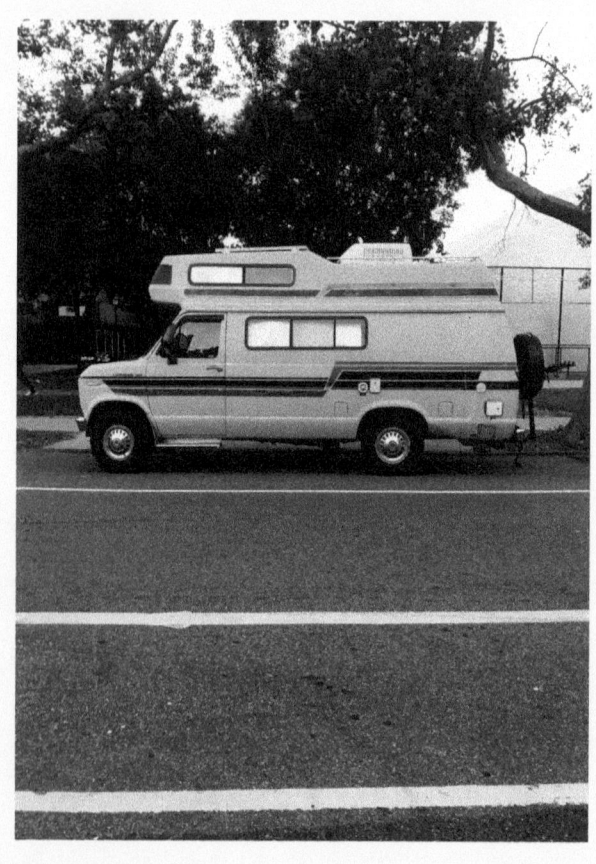

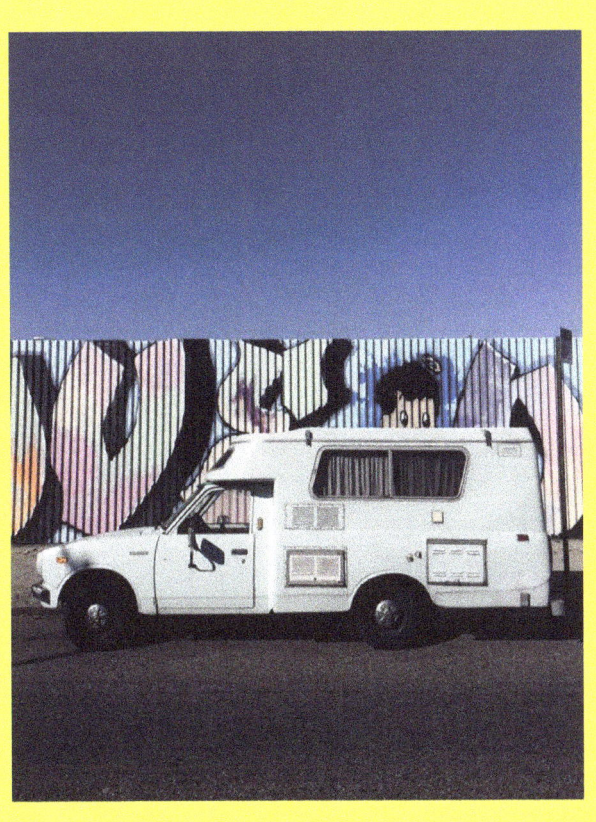

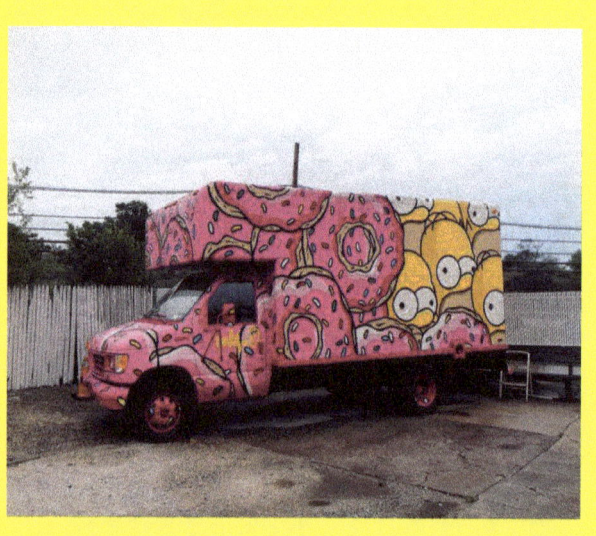

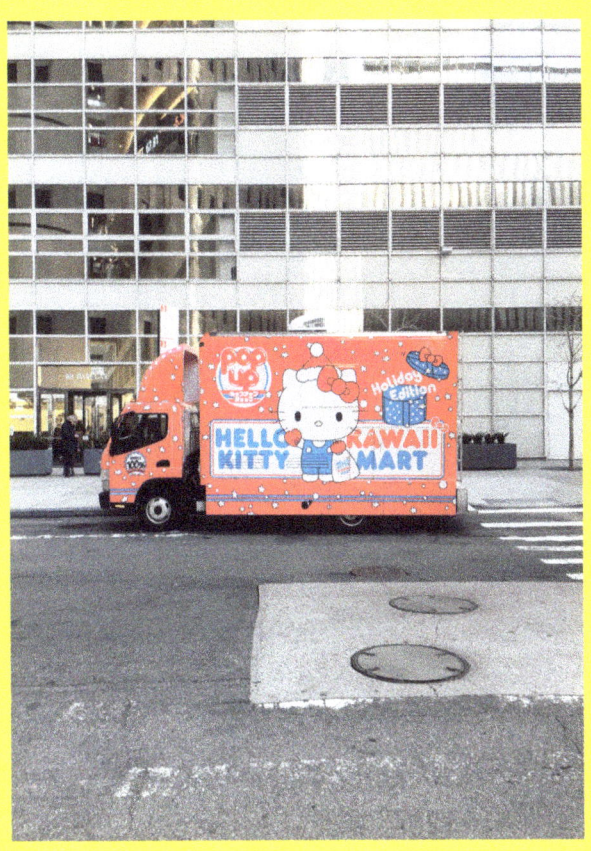

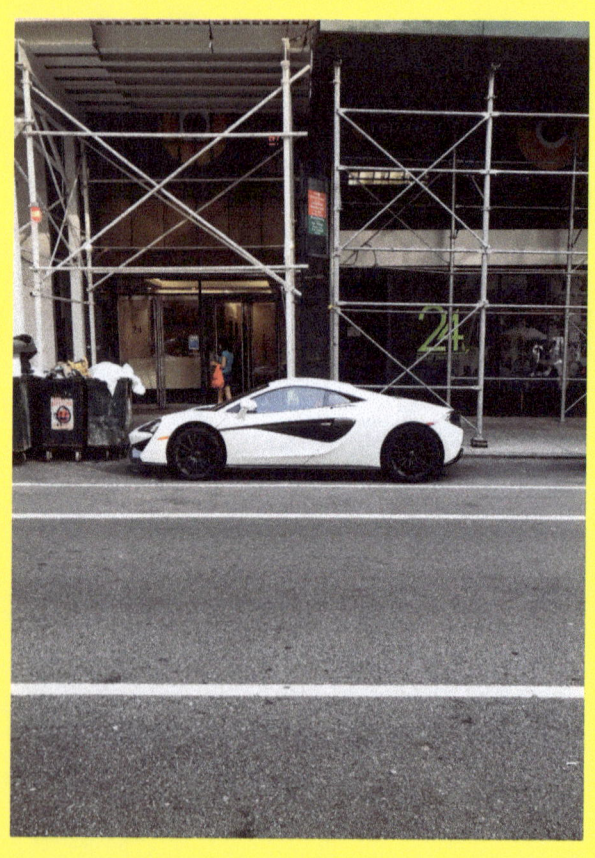

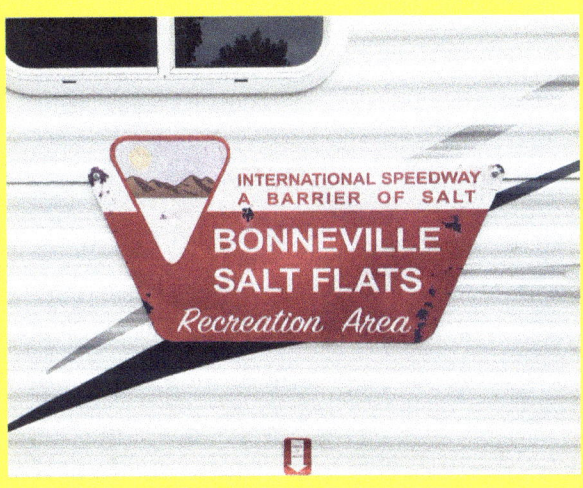

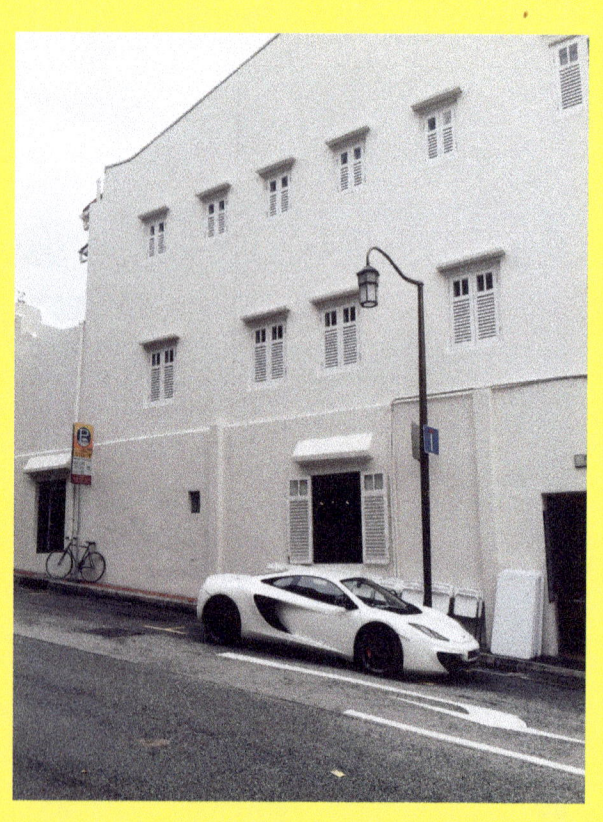

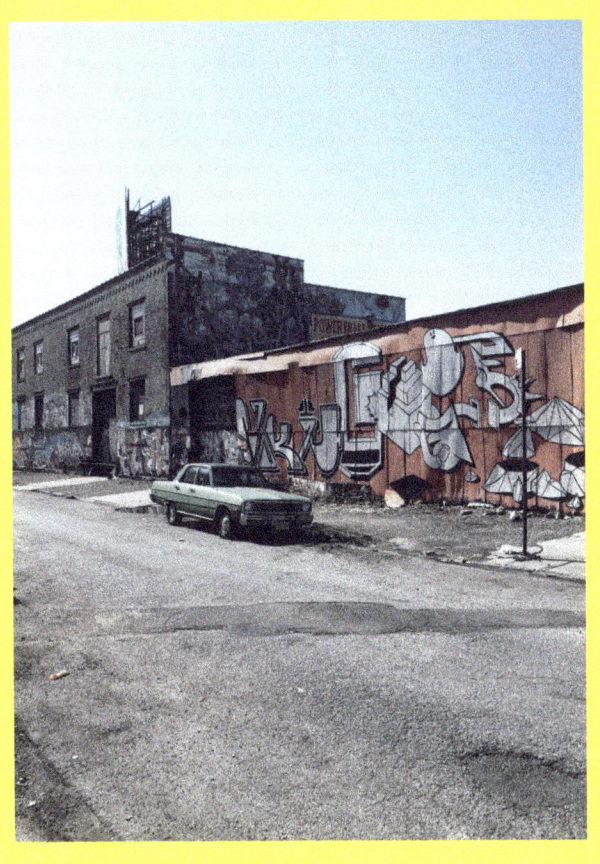

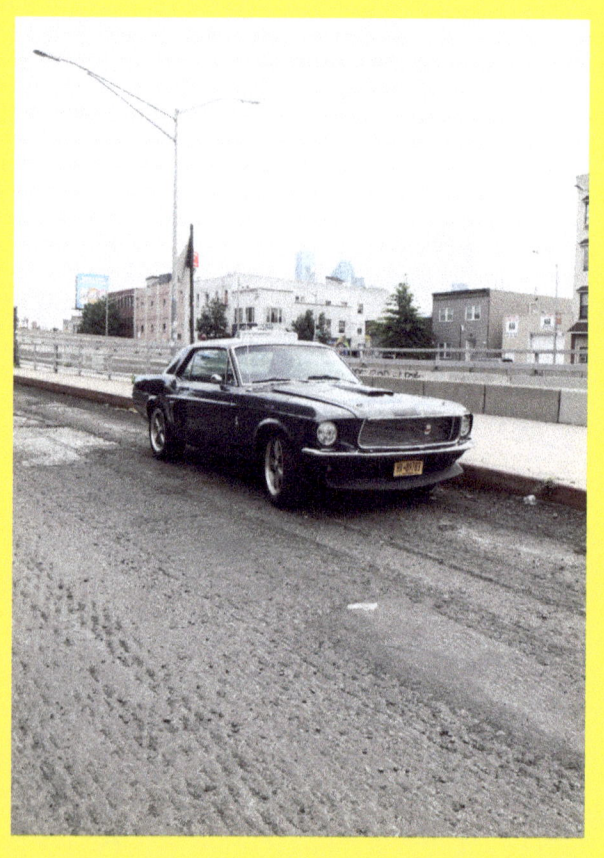

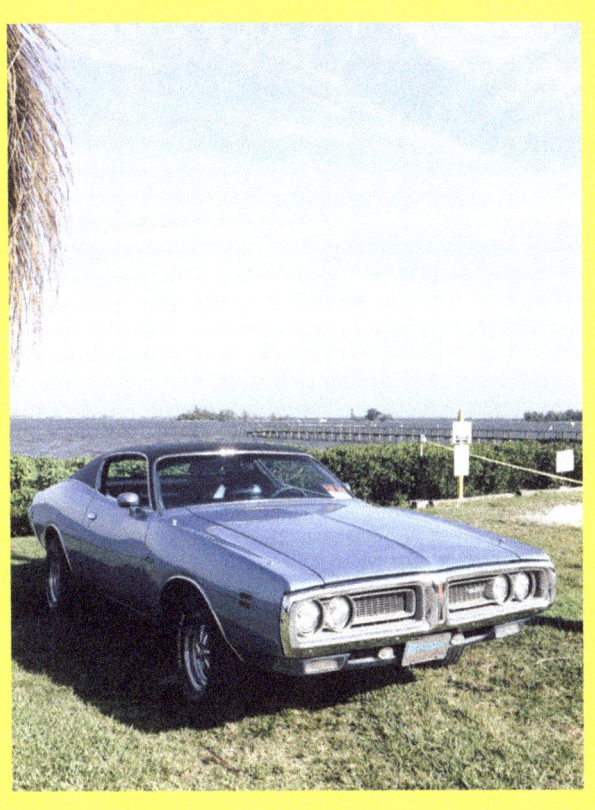

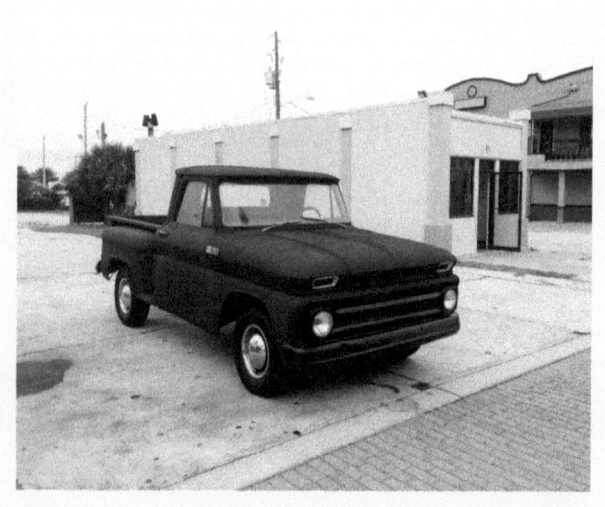

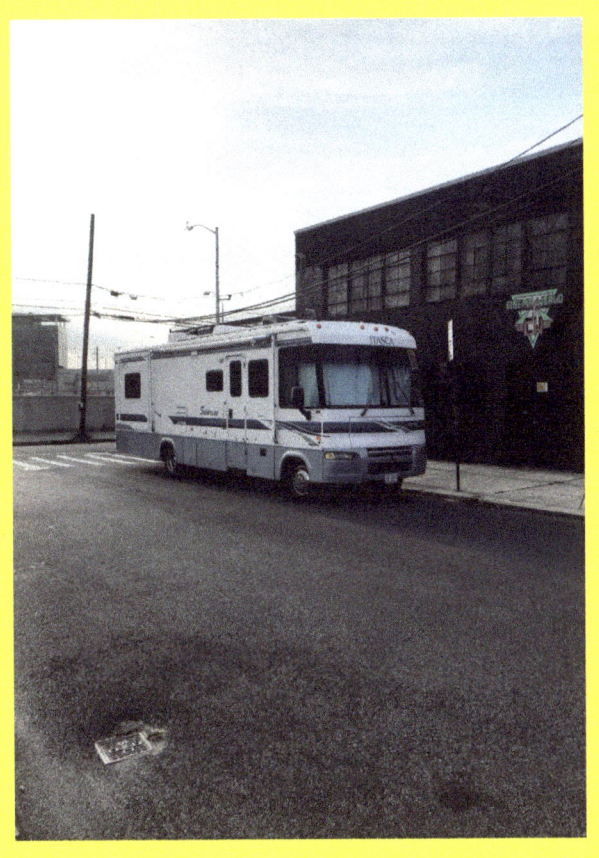

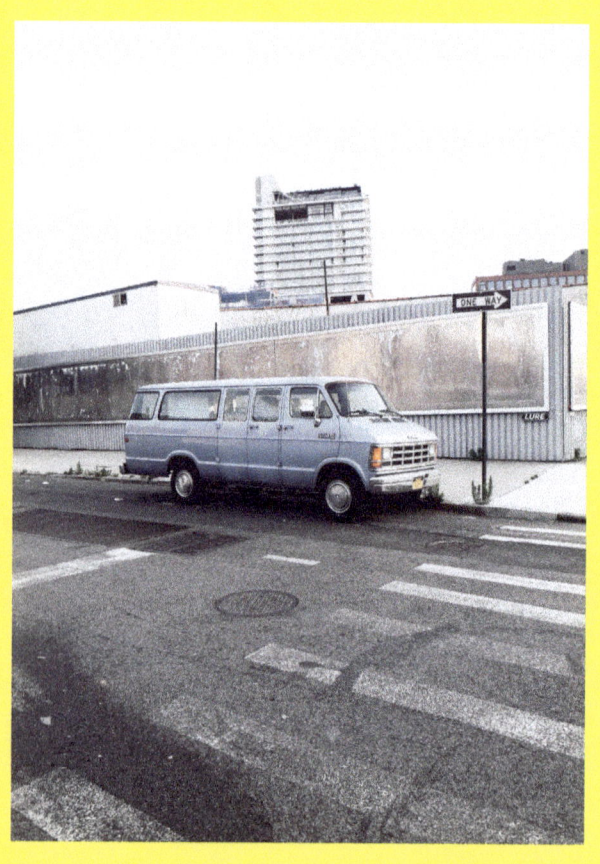

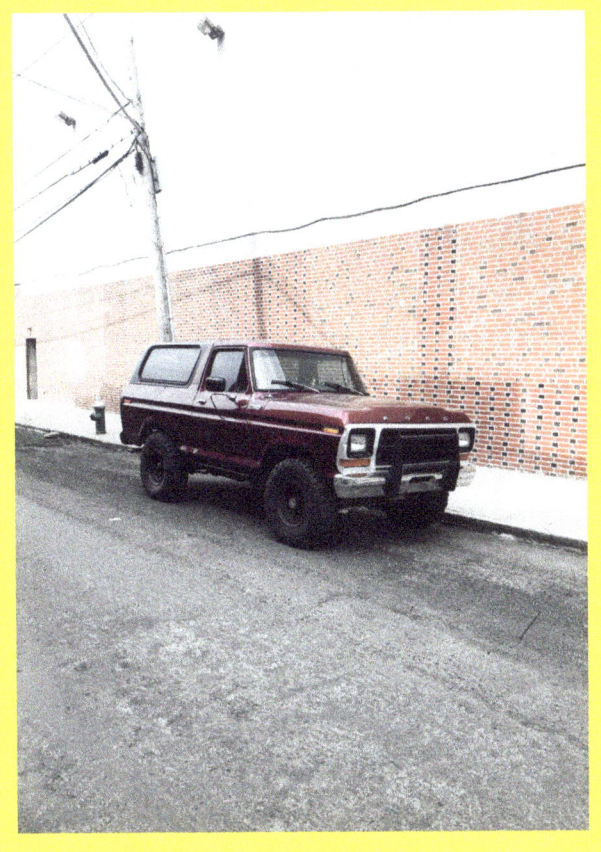

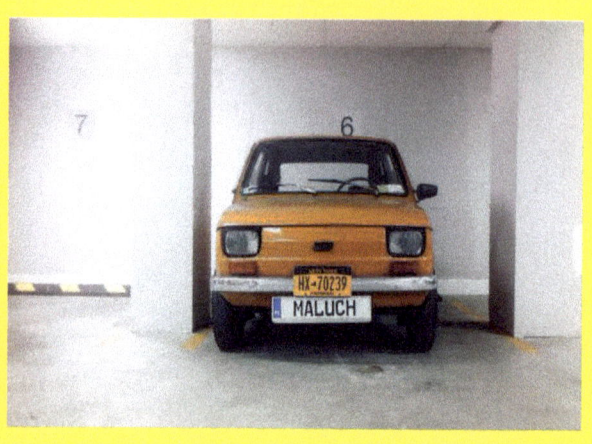

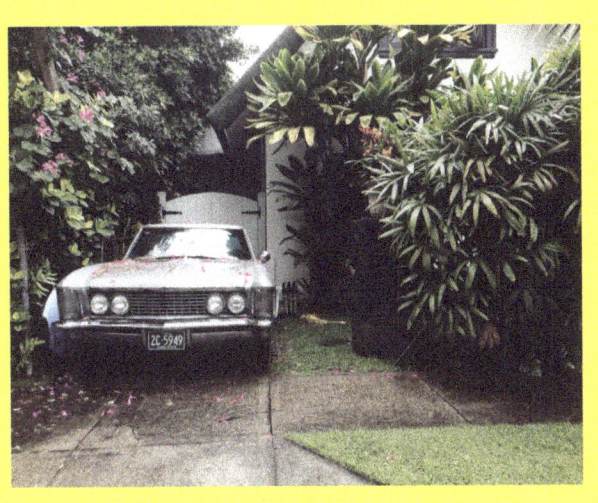

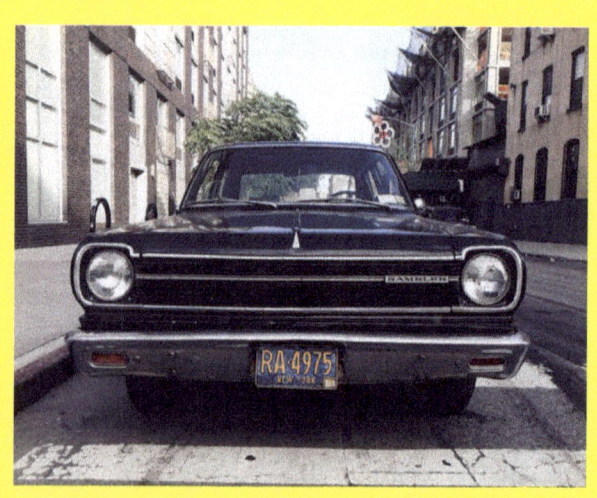

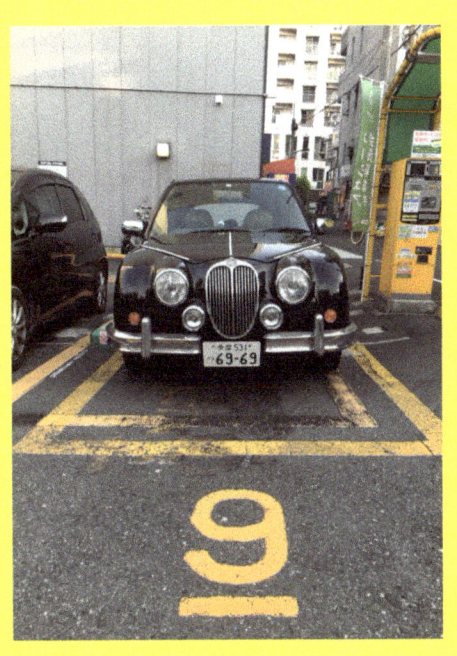

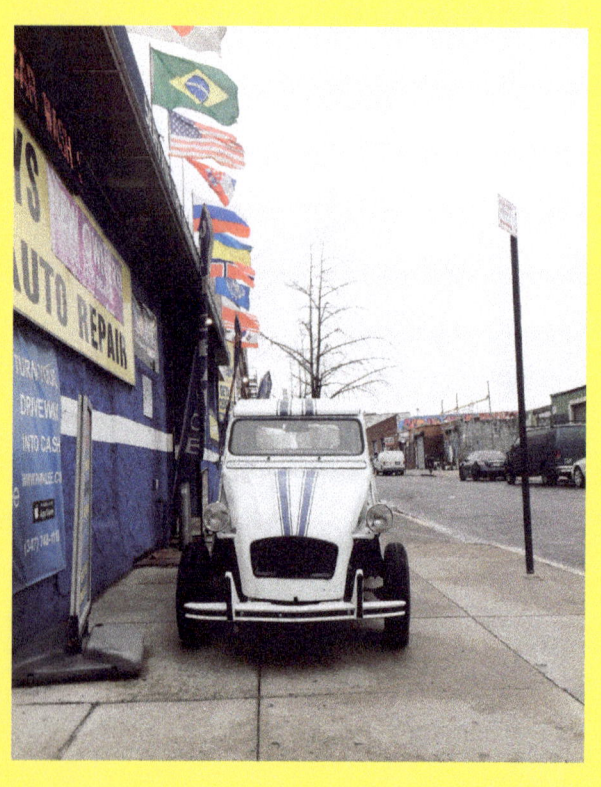

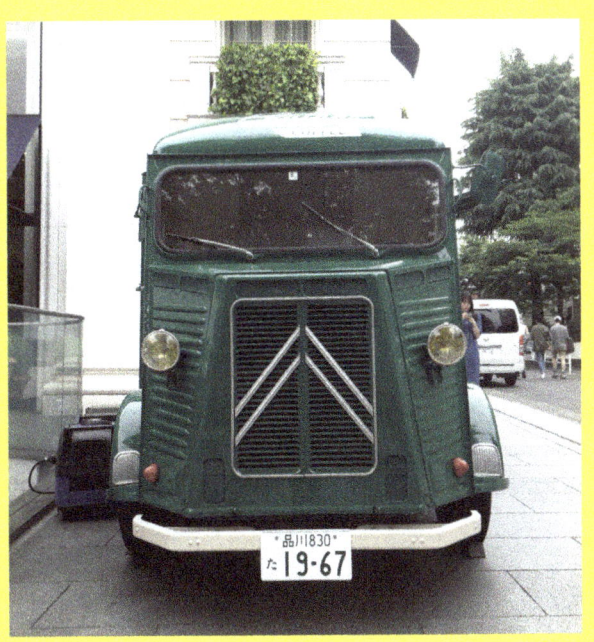

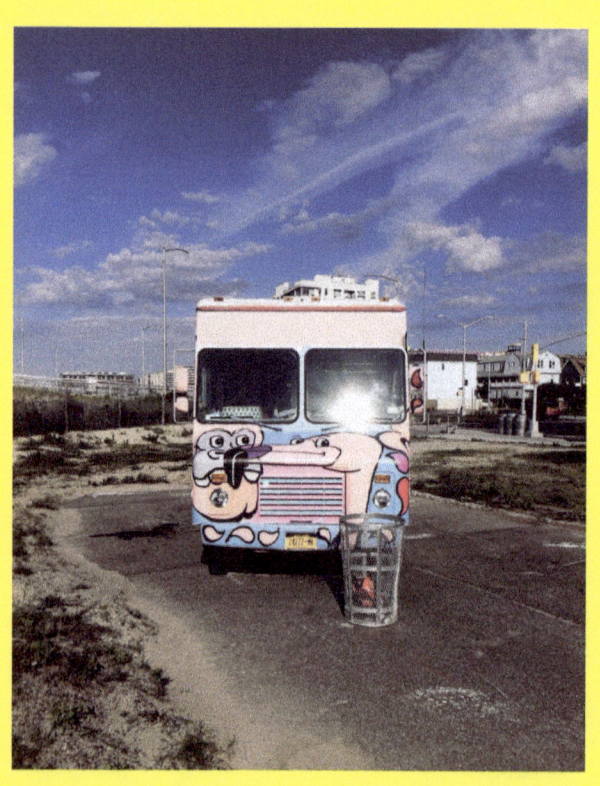

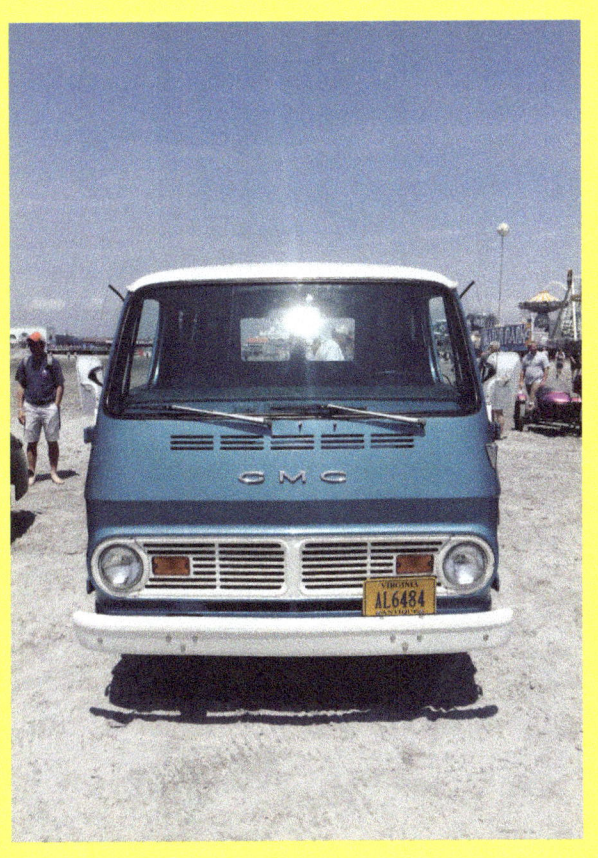

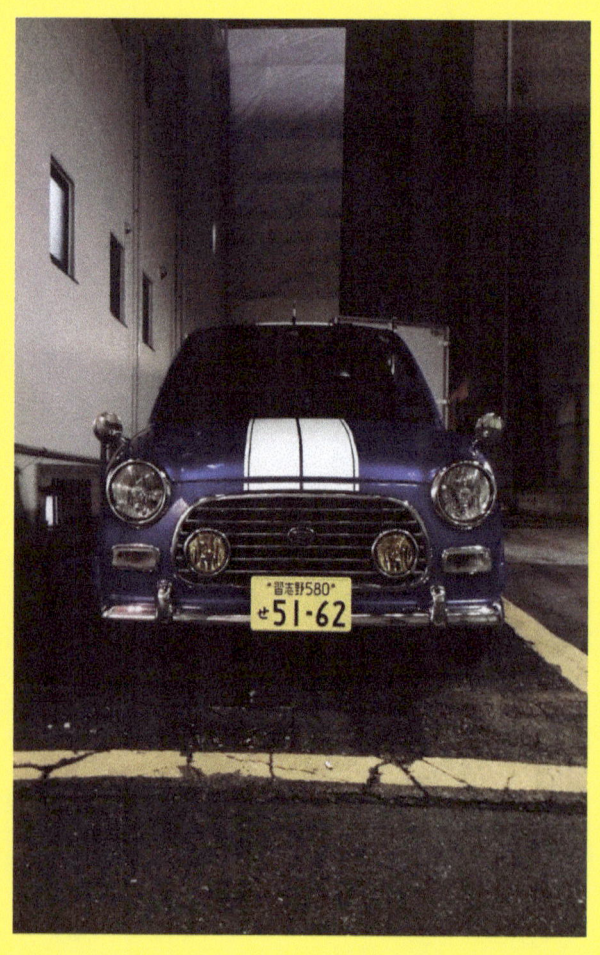

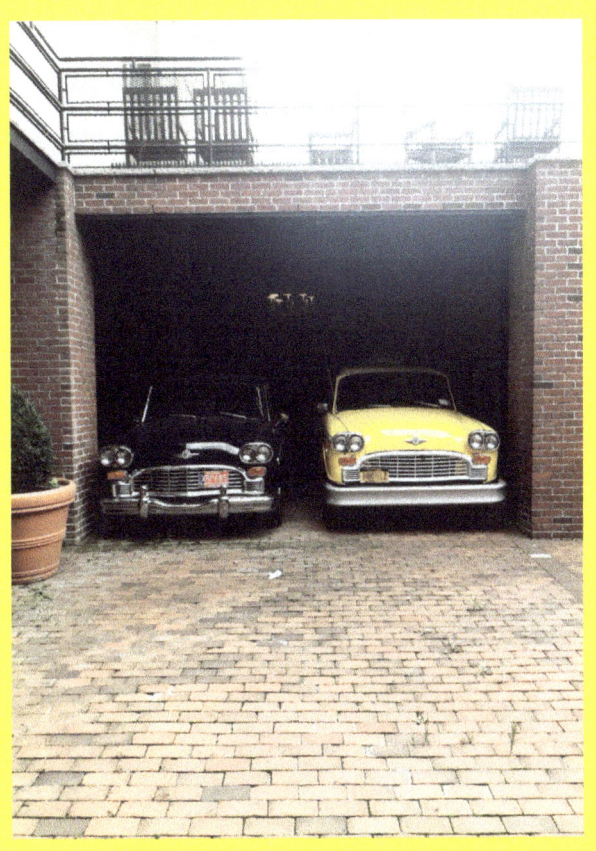

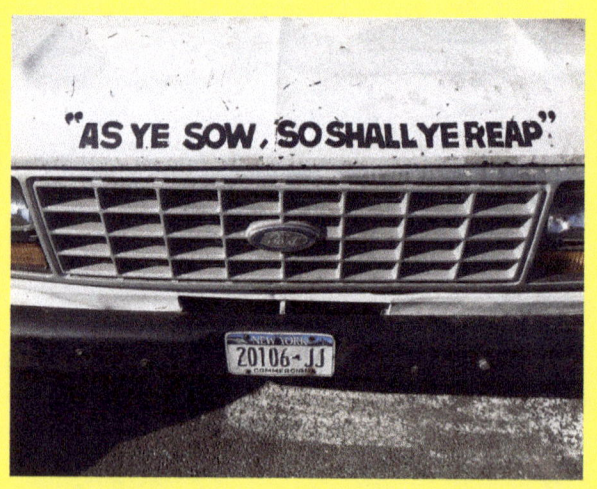

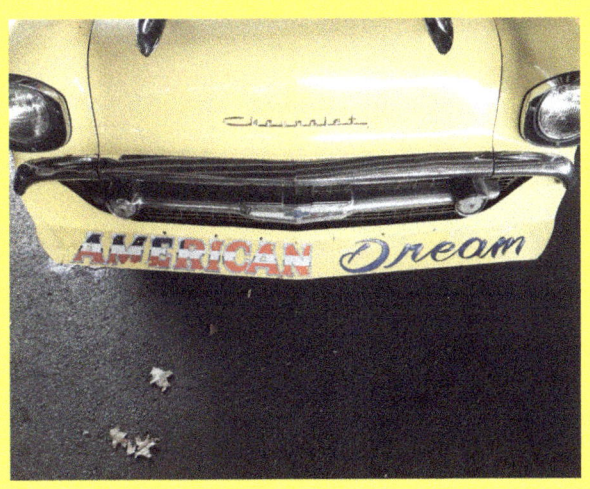

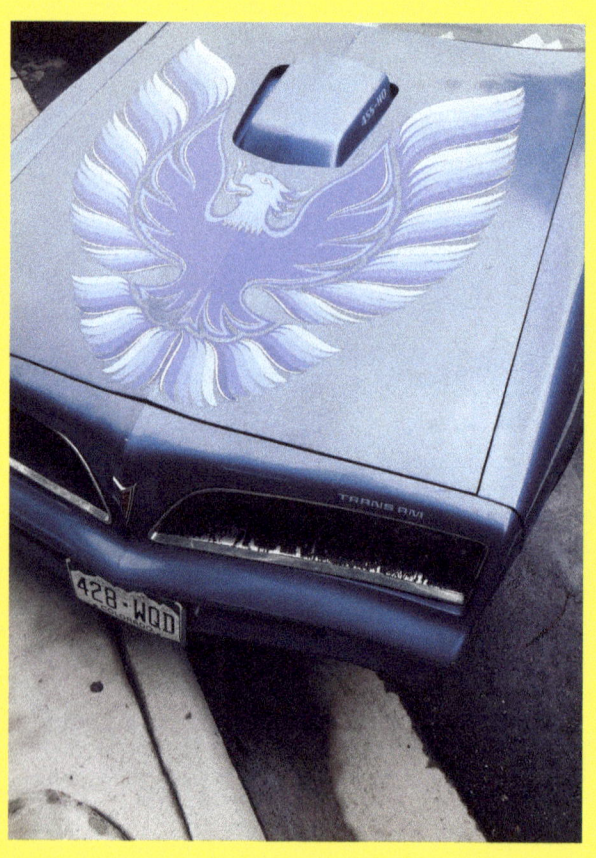

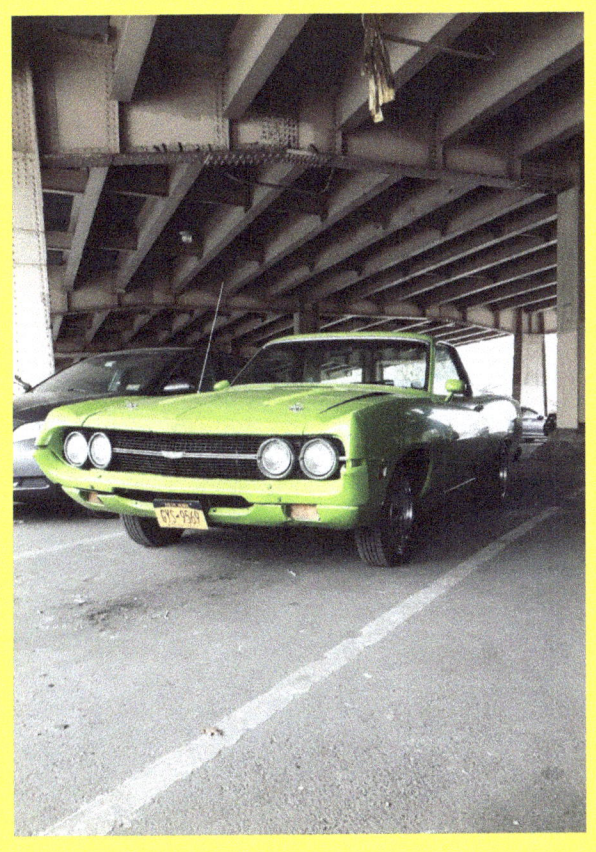

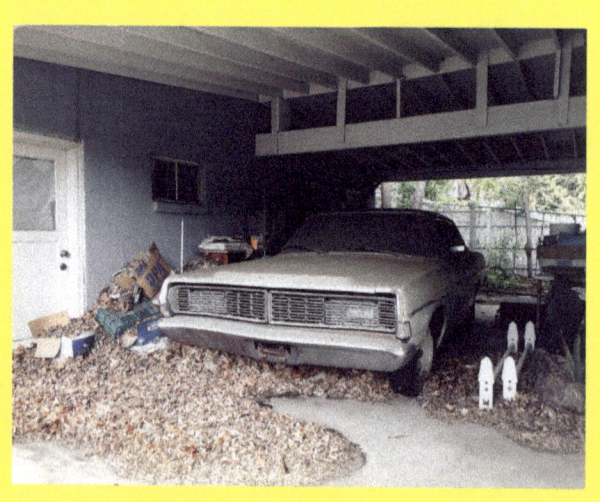

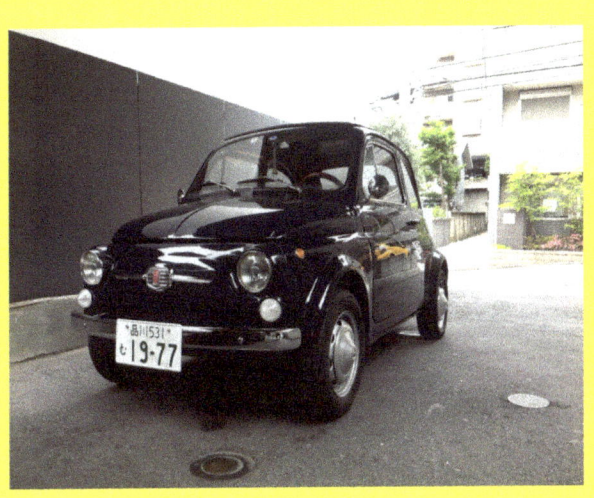

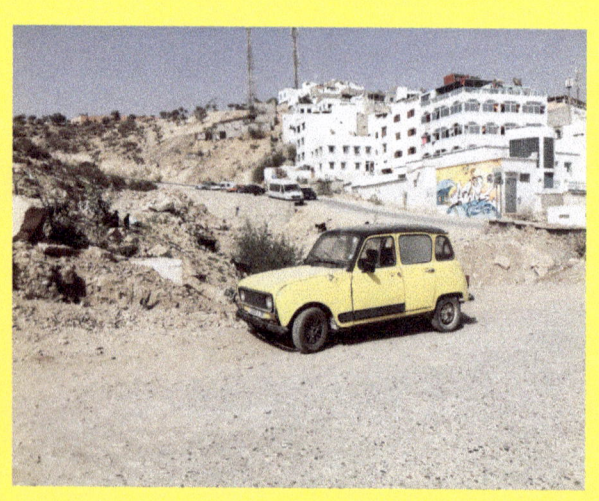

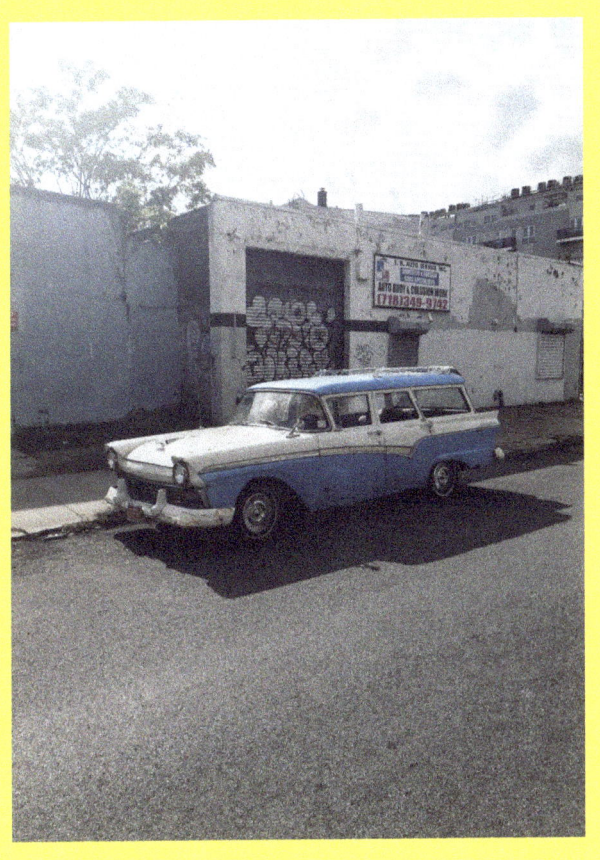

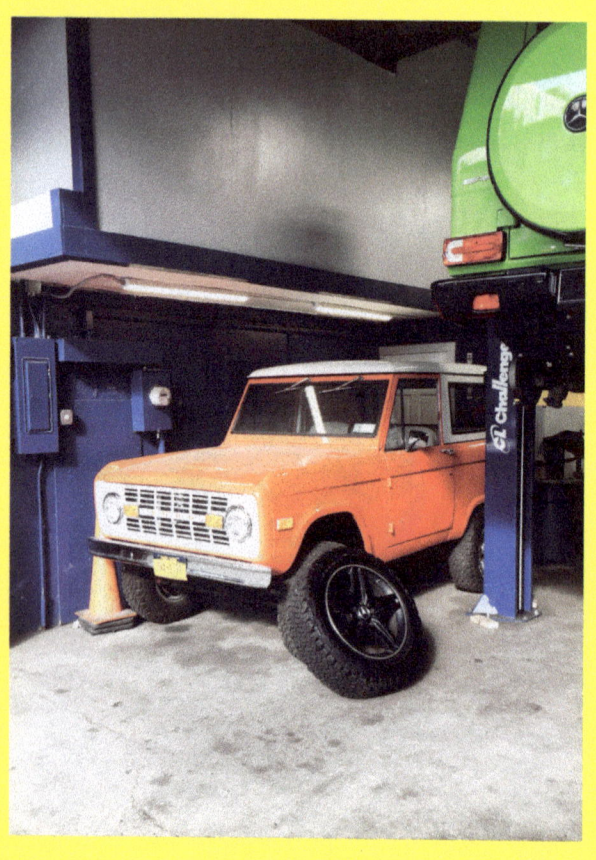

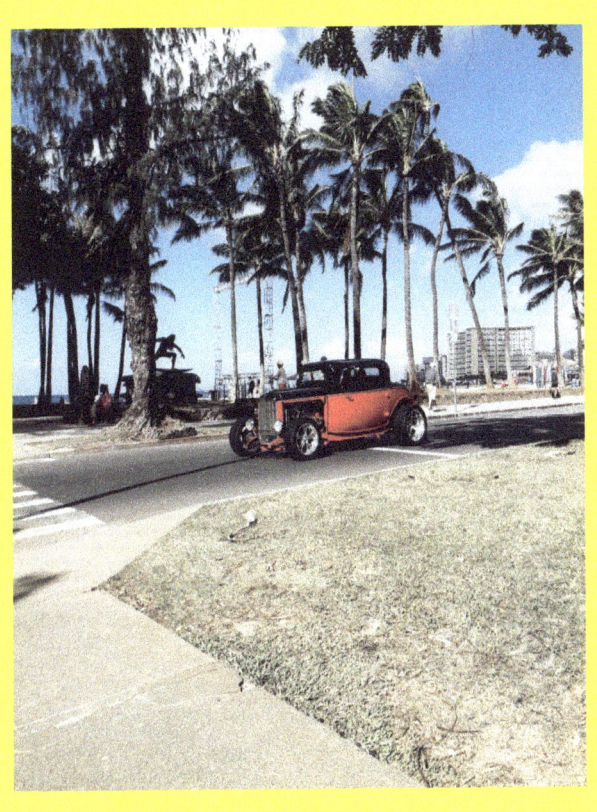

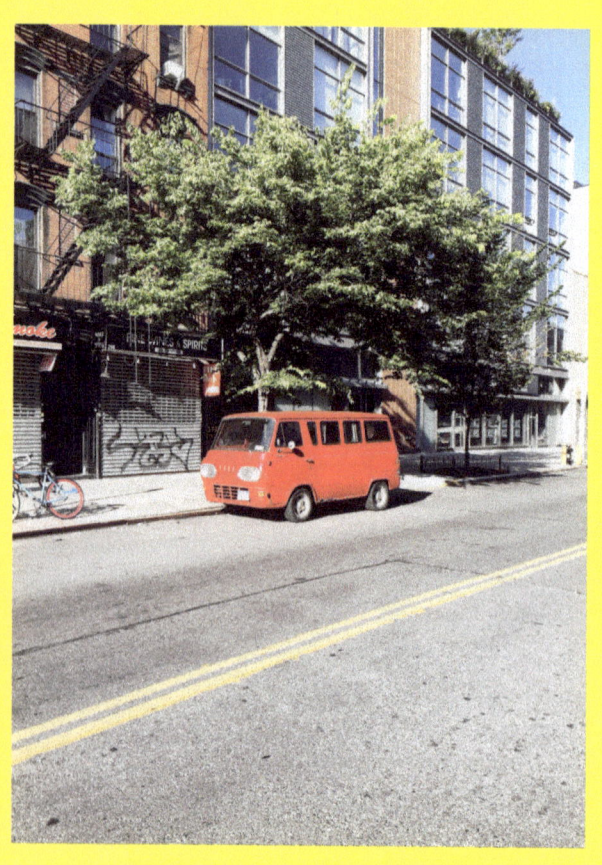

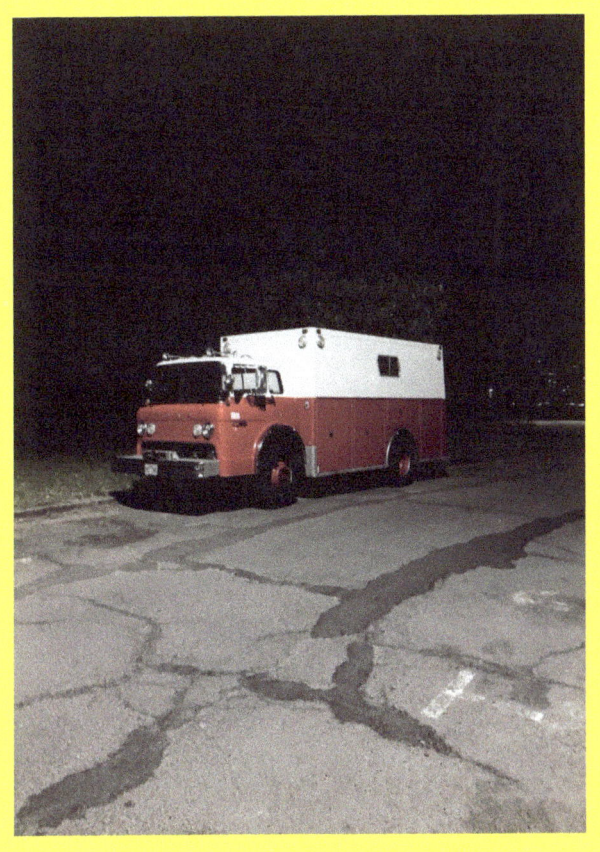

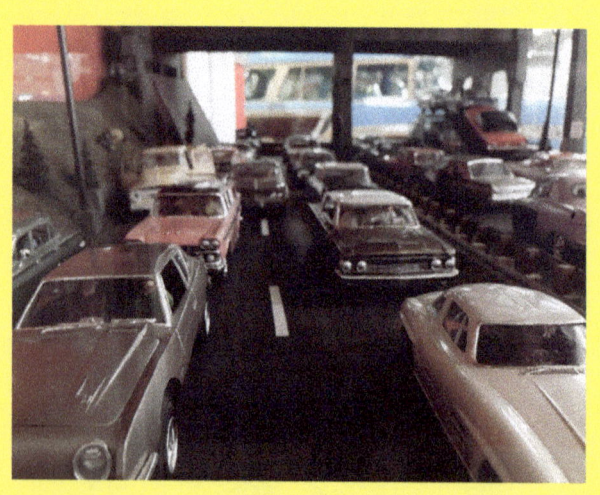

END

END

END

END

END

END

END

FAST DON'

FAST DON'T

E FAST DON'T

VE FAST DON'T S

RIVE FAST DON'T STO

DRIVE FAST DON'T STOP

DRIVE FAST DON'T STOP

DRIVE FAST DON'T STOP

DRIVE FAST DON'T STOP

WWW.DRIVEFASTDONTSTOP.COM

AUTOMOTIVE PHOTO ARCHIVE
BY
MATTHEW JOCELYN

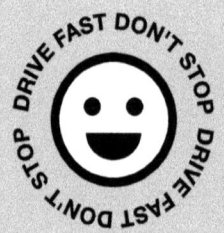

4